D1082894

A Gift For:

_____

From:

_____

The NOTICER

Sometimes, all a person needs is a little perspective.

ANDY ANDREWS

Dedicated to Polly . . . my wife, my best friend, my love . . . my noticer.

Chapter 1

His name was Jones. At least, that's what I called him. Not *Mr.* Jones . . . just Jones. He called me "young man" or "son." And I rarely heard him call anyone else by name either. It was always *young man* or *young lady*, *child* or *son*.

He was old, but the kind of old that is difficult to quantify. Was he sixty-five or eighty—or a hundred and eighty? And every single time I ever laid eyes on him, he had an old, brown suitcase close at hand.

Me? I was twenty-three when I saw him for the first time. He held out his hand, and for some reason, I took it. Looking back on the moment, I think that act in itself was a small miracle. Any other time, and with any other person, considering my circumstances, I might have cowered in fear or come out with my fists flying.

I had been crying, and he heard me, I guess. My cries were not the muffled sobs of loneliness or the whimpering of discomfort—though certainly I was lonely and uncomfortable—but the anguished wail that a guy will let loose only when he is sure there is no one around to hear him. And I *was* sure. Wrong, obviously, but sure. At least as sure as one spending another night under a pier can be.

My mother had succumbed to cancer several years earlier, a tragic event in my life that was compounded shortly thereafter by my father, who, neglecting to wear his seat belt, managed to chase my mother into the afterlife by way of an otherwise survivable automobile accident.

One questionable decision followed another during the confused aftermath of what I saw as "my abandonment," and within a couple of years, I found myself on the Gulf Coast, without a home, a vehicle, or the financial means to obtain either. I did odd jobs—mostly cleaning fish on the piers or selling bait to the tourists—and showered at the beach or swam myself clean in a pool at one of the hotels.

If it was cold, there was always a garage left open in one of the many empty vacation homes that dotted the beach. Rich people (anyone who owned a vacation home), I soon learned, often had an extra refrigerator or freezer hooked up in their garages. Not only were these excellent sources of old lunch meat and drinks, but they also worked almost as well as a heater if I lay close to the warm air that blew from the fan at the bottom.

Most nights, though, I much preferred my "home" underneath the Gulf State Park Pier. I had a large hole dug in and smoothed out right where the concrete met the sand. Visualize a monstrous lean-to: it was roomy, absolutely hidden from view, and as dry as anything ever is at the beach. I left my few belongings there—mostly fishing tackle, T-shirts, and shorts—often for days at a time, and never had anything stolen. Honestly, I didn't think anyone knew I slept there—which is why I was so surprised when I looked up and saw Jones.

"Come here, son," he said, with his hand outstretched. "Move into the light." I shuffled forward, taking his right hand with my own, and eased into the soft glow cast from the sodium vapor bulbs above the pier.

Jones was not a large man—nowhere near six feet—but neither was he small. His white hair was worn straight back over his head. It was too long, but had been carefully brushed and smoothed with his fingertips. His eyes, even in the dim light, seemed to shine. They were a clear, crystal blue, framed by a deeply wrinkled face. Though he wore jeans, a white T-shirt, and leather flip-flops, the old man seemed stately—though even now I admit that is hardly a word one would use to describe a five-foot-nine-or-so old man under a pier at night.

As I describe Jones, I might as well go ahead and tell you that I never knew whether he was black or white. I'm not sure it matters beyond trying to paint a mental picture for you, but I never asked and never decided if his café au lait–colored skin was the result of genetics or a life lived mostly outdoors. In any case, he was brown. Sort of.

"You crying about something in particular?" he asked. "Maybe some*body* in particular?"

Yeah, I thought. *Me. I am the "somebody in particular."* "Are you going to rob me?" I asked aloud. It was an odd question. More evidence, I suppose, of the level of distrust I had in everyone and everything at that time.

The old man's eyebrows rose. Peering beyond me into the darkness from which I had emerged moments before, he chuckled. "Rob you? I don't know . . . you got some furniture or a TV in there I didn't see?"

I didn't respond. I might have hung my head. Somehow, his attempt at humor made me feel worse. Not that he seemed to care.

He punched me playfully on the arm. "Lighten up, young man," he said. "First of all, you're about a foot and a half taller than me, so, no, I'm not about to rob you. Second . . . there is a benefit to not owning a bunch of stuff." I looked at him blankly, so he went on: "You're safe. Not only am *I* not gonna rob you; neither is anybody else. You got nothing to take!" He paused, aware that I was still not smiling. In fact, quite the opposite—I was becoming angry.

The old man changed tack. "Hey, Andy, if I promise not to *ever* rob you, can I have one of the Cokes you have stashed back in there?" He gestured behind me. I stared back at him. "Yes? No?" he said. "Please?"

"How did you know my name?" I asked.

"You can call me Jones, by the way."

"Okay. So how did you know my name? And how do you know whether or not I have any Cokes under here?"

"No big deal, really." He shrugged. "I been watching you for a long time. I been around. And the Cokes are bound to be a product of your late-night forays into the garages of the local rich and famous. So . . . can I have one?"

I watched him for a moment, considering his answer, then slowly nodded and retreated into the darkness for his Coke. Returning with two cans, I handed one to the old man.

"Didn't shake it up, did ya?" He grinned. Then, seeing once again that I refused even the slightest smile, he sighed and said, "Lord, Lord. You are a tough one." Popping the top on the Coke, Jones shifted in the sand and crossed his legs. "All right," he said, taking a long pull from the red can, "let's get started."

"Get started . . . at what?" I asked flatly.

Jones set his drink can down and said, "We need to start noticing a few things. We need to check your heart. We need to gather a little perspective."

"I don't even know what you are talking about," I said. "And I don't know who you are."

"Fair enough." He smiled. "Well, let me see, now . . . how do I explain?" He leaned toward me quickly. "As for who I am, call me Jo—"

"You already told me that," I interrupted. "What I mean—"

"Yeah, I know what you mean. You mean, where'd I come from, and stuff like that."

I nodded.

"Well, this evening, I came from just up the beach a ways." I sighed and rolled my eyes. Chuckling, he held up both hands in mock protest. "Hang on. Hang on, now. Don't get aggravated at old Jones." In a softer voice he added, "Okay?" Accepting my nod, he continued.

"I am a noticer," he said. "It is my gift. While others may be able to sing well or run fast, I notice things that other people overlook. And, you know, most of them are in plain sight." The old man leaned back on his hands and cocked his head. "I notice things about situations and people that produce perspective. That's what most folks lack—perspective—a broader view. So I give them that broader view . . . and it allows them to regroup, take a breath, and begin their lives again."

For several minutes we sat there quietly, peering out at the warm waters of the Gulf of Mexico. I was strangely calm in the presence of this old man, who was now lying on his side, elbow in the sand, with his head propped on his hand. After a while, he spoke again—a question this time. "So your mama and daddy passed on?"

"How did you know that?" I asked in return.

He gave the tiniest of shrugs, as if to say, *Everybody knows*, but I knew they didn't.

Though it alarmed me that this stranger seemed to know so much about me, I shook off the eerie feeling and answered his question. "Yeah, they're both dead."

He pursed his lips. "Well . . . that's a matter of perspective too." When I questioned him with a look, he continued. "There's a big difference in 'dead' and 'passed on.'"

"Not to me," I snorted.

"You ain't the one who's passed on."

"You got that right," I said bitterly. "I'm the one who's left." On the verge of tears again and with a mean tone of voice, I blurted out, "So what's your perspective on *that*? Huh?"

Carefully, Jones asked, "Well, why do you think you are here? In this situation . . . in this place, I mean."

"Because I chose to be," I tossed out. "My own bad decisions. My attitude." I stared hard at him. "See? I know all the right answers. So I don't need to hear it from you. It's all my fault, okay? Is that what you want me to say?"

"No," the old man said calmly. "I was just curious if you had any perspective of your own."

"Well, no, I don't," I said. "I grew up hearing that old adage about God putting a person after His own heart where He wants him to be. And He puts *me* under a pier?" I cursed, then added, "By the way, about that reference to the difference between 'dead' and 'passed on,' I've spent more than enough of my life in church, so I get what you're implying. I'm just not sure I buy any of that anymore."

"That's okay for the moment," Jones said soothingly. "I hear you. And I understand why you feel that way. But listen . . . I'm not selling anything. Remember, I am only here for—"

"For perspective, yeah, I know."

Jones was silent for a time, and I began to wonder if I had

been rude enough to shut him down completely. But, no. That was just the first of several chances I would offer him to give up on me and leave. And he didn't.

"Young man?" Jones asked as he brushed a wisp of white hair from his eyes. "What would you think if I told you that, yes, your bad choices and decisions have had a part in your ending up under this pier, but beyond that, under this pier is exactly where you should be in order for a future to occur that you can't even imagine at this point?"

"I don't understand," I said. "And I'm not sure I would believe it if I did."

"You will," Jones replied. "Trust me. One day you will." Then, suddenly smiling, he said, "Here's the thing, son, everybody seems to misunderstand that saying you threw at me a minute ago. Why does everyone think that when people say that 'God will put a person after His own heart where He wants him to be' . . . that it means God will put them on a mountaintop or in a big house or at the front of the line?

"Think with me here . . . everybody wants to be on the mountaintop, but if you'll remember, mountaintops are rocky and cold. There is no growth on the top of a mountain. Sure, the view is great, but what's a view for? A view just gives us a glimpse of our next destination—our next target. But to hit that target, we must come off the mountain, go through the valley, and begin to climb the next slope. It is in the valley that we slog through the lush grass and rich soil, learning and becoming what enables us to summit life's next peak.

"So, my contention is that you are right where you are supposed to be." The old man scooped up a double handful of the white sand and let it pour from his fingers. "It may look like barren sand to you, son, but nothing could be further from the truth. I say to you that, as you lay your head down tonight, you are sleeping on fertile ground. Think. Learn. Pray. Plan. Dream. For soon . . . you will *become*."

Before he left that night, Jones opened his suitcase, holding it carefully away from my curious gaze, and removed three small, orange hardcover books. "Do you read?" he asked. As I nodded, he added, "I'm not asking if you *can* read; I'm asking if you *do*."

"Yes," I responded. "Mostly magazines and stuff, but I do."

"Good enough," Jones said. "Read these."

I looked at what he handed me in the semidarkness. The titles were all names. *Winston Churchill. Will Rogers. George Washington Carver.* I glanced back up at him. "History books?"

"No," he said, with a twinkle in his eye, "adventure stories! Success, failure, romance, intrigue, tragedy, and triumph—and the best part is that every word is true! Remember, young man, experience is not the best teacher. *Other people's* experience is the best teacher. By reading about the lives of great people, you can unlock the secrets to what made them great."

I READ *Winston Churchill* UNTIL DAWN. IT WAS COMforting somehow to discover a life that had endured more tragedy and rejection than my own. And it didn't escape me that by the end of his life, Churchill had met with more than an equal measure of success.

Jones had said good-bye sometime after I started reading. I barely noticed him leave, but in the morning, I wished I had been nicer to the old man. I felt embarrassed, a bit ashamed of myself, but not nearly so devoid of hope as I had been the evening before. By nightfall, I had finished *George Washington Carver* and was so tired that I slept until the next morning.

That day, I washed boats at the marina and thought constantly about what I had read. I also kept an eye out for Jones, but I didn't see him. Gene, the marina manager, said he knew Jones well. He told me that the old man had been coming through town for years. "In fact," Gene said, "Jones was old when I was a boy. And I'm fifty-two."

I read *Will Rogers* within the next twenty-four hours, but it wasn't until several days later that I saw my friend again. I was throwing a cast net in the lagoon, trying to catch shrimp and mullet minnows to sell for bait, when the old man slipped up behind me. "Doing any good?" he asked.

"Hey, Jones!" I exclaimed. "I didn't hear you come up! Where've you been? I already read the books!"

He chortled at my enthusiasm. (Actually, I was a bit surprised myself that I was so glad to see him.) "Slow down, slow down! Let me comment." He grinned. "You didn't hear me come up because you were splashing around so much you wouldn't have heard me if I was riding an elephant. As for where I've been? I've been around—even seen you a couple of times—but didn't want to be a bother. And I'm glad you finished the books. Like 'em?"

"Yes, sir," I answered breathlessly. "I really did."

"Good. I figured you were through with all three by now. I hope you don't mind . . . I stopped by the pier and got them. And I left three more."

"Really?" I said, surprised. "Thanks."

"You're welcome. I'm getting them from the library. But I'm picking them out special for you." Jones then held up a plastic bag. "You hungry? I got lunch."

"I'm always hungry," I said. "Lately, I've been a 'one-meal-a-day' kind of guy, or what my mom used to call an 'opportunistic eater.'"

"Well, come on," he said. "Get out of the water. I have a feast."

The "feast" turned out to be Vienna sausages and sardines. I was hungry, so I ate, but I wasn't exactly thrilled with the fare, and Jones knew it. I wondered later if that's why he brought it in the first place.

We had settled under an oak tree on a high dune, the beach in front of us and the deep-blue lagoon at our backs. I wore old tennis shoes, blue jean cutoffs, and no shirt. Jones, in his usual casual attire, had coiled a blue bandanna around his head. The blue of that headband seemed to make his eyes glow. From where we sat, we could hear the crashing of the surf, and there was just enough breeze to make the summer temperature bearable. "So, what are you eating?" Jones asked, peering at me with a smile.

I looked up, puzzled. Wiping my mouth with the back of my hand, I swallowed and said, "What? You know what I'm eating. Same as you."

"Really?" the old man teased, with a sly look. "Somehow I doubt it. But let's see . . ." He leaned over to glance at my food, then looked back at me. "What are you eating?" he asked again. "And where are you eating it?" Seeing that I was now more confused than ever, he added gently, "It's not a trick; just answer the questions."

I raised my eyebrows and said, "Well . . ." I held up my hands as if to say, *I still don't know what you're getting at*, and said, "I guess I'm—"

"No, don't guess. Just tell me."

"Okay. I am eating sardines and Vienna sausages."

"Where?"

"In the sand."

Jones smiled. "I thought so." Nodding then, he said again, "I thought so. Well, the books will help, but I believe I can help as well."

"Jones," I said, shaking my head, "what are you talking about?"

"Your vision, my boy. It is incredibly cloudy at the moment, but I am certain we can clear a pathway from your head to your heart and into your future."

I was frustrated, but curious. "I still don't understand."

Jones put his hand on my shoulder and said, "I know you

don't. And I wouldn't expect you to understand." He leaned close to me. "Because you lack perspective."

He laughed at the expression on my face, but continued. "Young man, you see only the sand at your feet and what you are eating that you wish was something else. I don't tell you this as a rebuke; you are very ordinary in your views. Most people are just like you, disgusted with themselves for what they are and what they eat and what they drive. Most of us never stop to think that there are quite literally millions in this world who lack our blessings and opportunities, have no food to eat at all, and no hope of *ever* owning a car.

"The situation in which you find yourself is fraught with difficulty, yes. It is also piled high with benefits." Jones paused to ponder a thought, narrowed his eyes, then said, "Here, for you, young man, is a law of the universe—one of many, to be sure, but one that is especially applicable to your life at present. Remember, *whatever you focus upon, increases.*"

I frowned, trying to grasp the meaning of his words. Fortunately, Jones didn't leave me guessing.

"When you focus on the things you *need*," he went on to explain, "you'll find those needs increasing. If you concentrate your thoughts on what you *don't* have, you will soon be concentrating on other things that you had forgotten you don't have—and feel worse! If you set your mind on loss, you are more likely to lose . . . But a *grateful* perspective brings happiness and abundance into a person's life."

Jones saw the doubt on my face. He put his cans aside and shifted his body to face me directly. "Consider this: when we are happy and enthusiastic," he said, "other people enjoy being around us. True?"

"I guess," I answered.

"No guesses," Jones chided. "When we are happy and enthusiastic, other people enjoy being around us. Yes or no?"

"Yes."

"And knowing that one's opportunities and encouragement *come* from people, what happens to a person everyone enjoys being around?"

I was beginning to catch on. "They get more opportunities and encouragement?" I ventured.

"That is correct," Jones affirmed. "And what happens to a life filled with opportunities and encouragement?" As I opened my mouth to speak, the old man answered for me. "A life filled with opportunities and encouragement finds more and more opportunities and encouragement, and success becomes inevitable."

Seeing the hope and new understanding in my expression, Jones held up a finger. "I must caution you, however," he said, "that the opposite of this principle is true as well. When a person is negative, complaining, and disagreeable, other people stay away. And that person receives *less* encouragement and fewer opportunities—because no one wants to be around him. And we know what happens to a life without opportunities and encouragement . . ."

"Things get worse and worse," I answered.

Jones paused a moment to let the truth of my last realization sink in. Then he offered a plan of action. "So how *does* one become a person whom other people want to be around? Let me make a suggestion. Ask yourself this question every day: 'What is it about me that other people would change if they could?'"

Thinking for a moment, I had a question of my own. "Jones, what if I get an answer about something that I don't want to change?"

The old man tittered and replied, "The question wasn't about *you* in the first place. The question was, what would *other* people change about you if they could?"

Sensing my uncertainty, he explained, "Look, son, I'm not saying that you should live your life according to the whims of others. I am simply pointing out that if you are to become a person of influence—if you want people to believe the things you believe or buy what you are selling—then others must at least be comfortable around you. A successful life has a great deal to do with perspective. And another person's perspective about you can sometimes be as important as your perspective is about yourself."

For several minutes, we both sat silently, watching the gulls soar overhead, listening to the surf break on the beach. Then Jones began to gather the empty cans and place them in the plastic bag. Standing, he extended his hand and helped me to my feet. "Incidentally," he said with a smirk, "*you* ate sardines and Vienna sausages in the sand. *I* dined on surf and turf with an ocean view." He slapped me on the back. "It's all about perspective."

LATER THAT DAY, I CRAWLED BACK INTO MY HOME UNDER the pier. Laid neatly on my tackle box were three more orange books. Again, they were all biographies. Joan of Arc. Abraham Lincoln. Viktor Frankl. I picked up the Frankl book first; I was unfamiliar with him. The book was titled *Man's Search for Meaning*. As I skimmed through, I learned that Frankl was an Austrian psychiatrist who survived the Nazi death camps during World War II. His wife, father, and mother were all murdered.

It's all about perspective . . . I could hear Jones's voice rattling around in my head.

Suddenly I noticed that there was a piece of paper folded into the book. As I removed it, I could see that it was a napkin. On it, Jones had written:

> Young man,
> Read this one first. I am proud of you.
> Jones

Tears filled my eyes as I carefully placed the letter back into the book. It had been a long time since anyone had been proud of me.

TODAY, I CAN REMEMBER DISTINCTLY THAT THE NEXT three books were *Harry Truman, Florence Nightingale,* and *King David.* Then I was given *Harriet Tubman, Queen Elizabeth I,* and *John Adams.* Numbers thirteen, fourteen, and fifteen were *Eleanor Roosevelt, Mark Twain,* and *Joshua Chamberlain.* Tucked into the Chamberlain book was a note from Jones, simply instructing me to please return these last three to the library myself, which I did—and I checked out *George Washington, Anne Frank,* and *Christopher Columbus* on my own.

It wasn't long before I noticed that Jones had gone.

I looked for him for weeks, finding evidence of his having "been around" at every turn. Jones had arranged for Nancy, the owner of Sea N Suds, a restaurant on the beach, to fry any fish I brought in. Hush puppies and iced tea were included in my special price. Along with all the crackers I could eat, the price was a dollar.

Soon, more charter boat captains began giving me their boats to wash, and in some cases, their clients' fish to clean. Every single time, Jones's name was mentioned.

One day, Brent Burns, a songwriter performing at the Holiday Inn, told me that an old man had informed him that I was funny and had suggested that I might do some comedy during his breaks. Could I? he asked. I did, and though I was probably not very good, Brent laughed at my material several times a week and encouraged me with his words and an occasional meal.

THE NEXT SEVERAL YEARS WERE A BLUR. I CONTINUED TO read biographies even though the pier was no longer my shelter. Through the influence of General George Patton, Madame Curie, Joshua, Caleb, Harriet Beecher Stowe, Alexander the Great, Booker T. Washington, Daniel Boone, and eventually more than two hundred other biographies, I had begun to move my life in a forward direction.

At some point during that time, a crystallizing moment occurred as I read yet another account of the life of some influential, financially secure, highly successful person. I realized that a graph had formed in my mind, unconsciously identifying seven things that these great people all had in common—seven principles they had all employed. And I wondered, *What would happen to my life if I harnessed the power of these seven principles? After all,* I reasoned, *principles work every time. And they work whether I understand them or not. The principle of gravity was working long before the apple ever fell on Newton's head . . . yet when that apple finally did fall, and Newton understood the principle behind it, society was then free to harness that principle to fly airplanes, build suspension bridges, and a host of other things!*

Continuing this line of thought, I became convinced that the principles of personal success—in parenting, finances, leadership, and relationships—are no different from the principle of gravity. *And since they do work every time, and they work whether or not I know them,* I concluded, *why shouldn't I harness them and apply them in my daily life, to create the future God wants for me?*

So I did.

My life today, the well-being of my family, and whatever success we have enjoyed have been direct results of the power of seven simple principles. Several years ago, I shared these principles with the world, in a book that became a *New York Times* Best Seller and has since been translated into more than twenty languages. *The Traveler's Gift* is now used by corporations, teams, governments, and individuals all across the globe.

The Traveler's Gift is a story about a family enduring a tragic period in their lives. As the story progresses, the father, David Ponder, is allowed to travel through time, meeting with seven historic individuals who are also experiencing turmoil and hardship. These people—among them Harry Truman, Anne Frank, Abraham Lincoln, King Solomon, and Columbus—each give Ponder a separate principle to incorporate into his life. And because of these seven principles, his life is changed forever.

SO, IF YOU HAVE EVER HEARD ME SPEAK AT A CORPORATE event or read any of my books and wondered how I came to read more than two hundred biographies—books that led me to the seven principles—now you know. It was an old man named Jones who took an interest in (or pity on) a young man going through the worst time in his life.

I have thought of Jones every single day now for almost twenty-five years. On the day I was married, I had hoped he would be there. I wanted him to sit in the first row—where my father would have been. When each of my boys was born, I walked outside the hospital alone, in the half-light of an early morning, hoping to find Jones waiting, smiling, ready with advice and comfort about my future as a father. There have been so many times I've wished for just an hour alone with that old man. But I never saw him again.

Until last week.

Chapter 2

TO TELL THE TRUTH, I'D BEEN DOING A DOUBLE TAKE AT every white-haired old man I had seen for more than two decades, hoping it was Jones, but I was always disappointed. I tried to tell myself that it didn't make sense . . . he was an old man *then*. How much older would he be by now? I finally decided that Jones was no longer alive—couldn't be.

But then, last Thursday, just past noon, I was in Sea N Suds—the same restaurant I used to visit for a dollar. It is still owned by Nancy and still "my lunch place," even though she charges me full price now. I was eating a shrimp sandwich at the oyster bar and teasing Willie, who was shucking oysters, when Nancy walked over. "Hi, Nancy," I said.

"Hi, yourself," she replied with a smile. "Is Willie bothering you?"

"Yes," I said, laughing. "Willie is always bothering me."

"Come on, now!" Willie protested as he popped another oyster open and put it on a plate. "Be good to Willie. There's plenty of *nice* people waiting for that stool."

We laughed, but as I looked around, I could see he was right. Spring break was in full swing, and in Gulf Shores, that meant that the little restaurant overlooking the water was packed. There were even people sitting outside, waiting for a table or for room to open up at the bar.

"It's good to see your buddy again," Nancy said. "Do you want some more iced tea?"

"Thanks," I said, pushing the plastic glass across to her. "What buddy? Who'd you see?"

"Jones," she answered, nodding her head to a point somewhere behind me. "He came in a few minutes ago with Jan and Barry Hanson." Nancy saw the stunned expression on my face—maybe the beginning of tears in my eyes as I quickly searched the restaurant—and she offered an awkward apology. "I'm sorry I didn't say anything when he came in . . . I guess he didn't see you either; you have your back to the door. I just assumed you two were . . . you know . . . together."

I spotted him at the southwest corner table, with his back to me, but there was no mistaking all that white hair and the brown suitcase on the floor beside him. It *was* Jones. I had to stop myself from running across the restaurant and yelling his name.

"How long has it been since he was here?" Nancy asked. "Seems like forever, but he sure looks the same."

He did look the same. His hair was cut a bit shorter perhaps, but not much. It was still worn a bit carelessly and he was still in jeans. Even the leather flip-flops looked like the same ones—but surely they weren't.

I eased gingerly between tables, moving to see him from the side before I approached. After all this time, I still couldn't believe it was him. Jan and Barry, a couple I knew, saw me first, and Barry stood, calling my name in greeting. It was obvious I was headed for their table, and I suppose they assumed I wanted to talk to them. And any other time I would have. This time, however, I was in some degree of shock—and they were not my object of interest.

I came closer and despite the loud voices all around us, quietly said, "Jones?" He turned and smiled. "Oh, man," I said, sinking to my knees in order to hug him before he could even get up, "I can't believe it's you. I can't . . . where have you been? I thought maybe you were dead. I'm so . . . hey, I have a wife and two boys."

"I know, I know," he said as he hugged me. "Slow down. We have plenty of time to talk."

I was suddenly embarrassed, realizing that several people around us were looking. Even the Hansons seemed ill at ease, though for some reason I didn't feel it had anything to do with me.

"Do you know each other?" Jan asked.

Considering the circumstances, it was one of the dumber questions I've heard in my life, but I felt it was not my place to tell her at that moment. Normally, *No, I do this to every old man I see* is what I would have said, but just this once, I kept my sarcasm buttoned down and managed a simple, "Yes." Then I added, "Jones is the single person on this planet most responsible for my—"

"I met Andy when he was a much younger man," Jones interrupted forcefully, but in a cheerful voice. Addressing me then, he said with a chuckle, "You're not quite as skinny as you used to be."

"No sir," I responded. "I eat a little more regularly now."

"Good food?" he asked with a twinkle in his eyes.

"Jones, it's all surf and turf, with an ocean view."

"Good man," he said as he reached out and squeezed my arm. "Can I meet you somewhere later?"

I was suddenly aware that Jan and Barry were looking extremely uncomfortable, though for the life of me, I couldn't imagine why. "Yes. Sure," I said. "Do you want me to wait outside, or . . . ?" I gestured a *whatever-you-want-me-to-do* with my hands.

"Tell you what," Jones said, "I want to talk to my new best friends a bit. Meet me at our old place in a couple of hours, but on top of the pier this time, okay?" He winked at me. "I think I'll impose on these fine folks to drop me off . . . or maybe they'll walk me there." The Gulf State Park Pier, my old home, was only a mile or so up the beach. In fact, we could see it from Sea N Suds.

"Sounds good," I answered. "See you in a couple of hours, then."

As I said good-bye to the Hansons, I couldn't help but notice, again, that they (Barry, especially) looked as if they were about to bolt. And had Jones said they were his *new best friends*? What did that mean?

FORTY-FIVE MINUTES EARLIER, BARRY HANSON HAD walked out of his attorney's office in a daze. After twenty-one years of marriage, Jan had filed for divorce. She still loved him; she just didn't like him anymore. She didn't *feel* loved, she had said.

Barry was the president of the local branch of the state's largest bank. He made a good salary and had saved wisely, and, while not what one might call rich, his family was debt free and very comfortable. He was an active member of several civic organizations and served on two committees at his church. Furthermore, by all accounts, Barry was a great father to his two children: Elizabeth, fourteen; and Jared, ten.

Jan stopped teaching full-time when Jared was born, and directed her energy toward Barry, their children, and volunteer work in the Gulf Shores / Orange Beach area. She was slender, wore her dark hair short, and was one of the more popular ladies in the community. Jan also sang in the Coastal Chorale, an auditioned community choir.

Jan and Barry were the same age—forty-three—and had attended the same university, though they had not met until two years after graduation, at the wedding of a mutual friend.

They fell madly in love, couldn't imagine an hour (let alone their whole *lives*) without each other, and were married within the year.

Now Barry could not imagine what had gone wrong. He loved Jan. He had always loved her, though from time to time he grew irritated at her because she never seemed to believe it. How many times had he said, "I love you," or "You're beautiful," only to see her eyes narrow in suspicion or tear up in disbelief? Privately, it drove him nuts. But he *did* love her. And now this? *Divorce?* He could hardly believe it.

IT WAS ALMOST NOON. AS JAN MOVED THROUGH THE house, picking up here and there, she kept an eye on the clock. She was meeting Barry for lunch, perhaps for the last time. No, that wasn't true, she told herself; there were the children to consider. She had told him she wanted a divorce two days ago, and neither of them had slept since.

Gathering her purse and keys, Jan walked out onto their front porch and locked the door behind her. As she moved toward the steps, she paused—almost stopped—and shook her head at the holly bush that threatened to overgrow the sidewalk in front of her. Wiping tears from her eyes, Jan set her jaw and strode purposefully to the car. For more than a year—*a year*— she had mentioned that holly bush to her husband. But had he trimmed it? No. He had not. Neither had he fixed the back screen door or painted the carport, like she had asked.

Jan backed the car out into the street, put the car in drive, accelerated—and immediately slammed on the brakes. There was an old man in front of her. She had not hit him—had not even come close, but he'd scared the daylights out of her.

It was Jones, the old man who wandered in and out of town every now and then. He had been doing something at the Shearsons' house down the street for several days, and she had noticed him walking through the neighborhood the afternoon before. Jan had never talked to the old man, but knew quite a few people who had. And everyone, as far as she knew, loved him.

"I am so sorry," he said as he came around to the driver's side window. "I didn't mean to scare you. I tried to get your attention as you were backing up."

"Oh, gosh!" Jan said, catching her breath. "I'm sorry too. I guess I wasn't paying attention like I should have. I'm just . . . well . . . I have some other things on my mind. Did you want something?"

"Yes," the old man smiled. "May I ask if you are headed to the beach?" Jan nodded hesitantly as he continued. "I don't mean to impose, but could I have a ride? I'm afraid I am going to be late for a lunch appointment." He paused, noticing her indecision, then with a tilt of his head and an expression of humility, added, "Please?"

Ordinarily, Jan wouldn't have given a ride to anyone she didn't know, not in a million years. But this old man seemed safe. "Okay," she said, wondering vaguely what Barry would say about her giving a ride to a stranger, then decided it didn't matter anymore. "Hop in. Do you need to put your suitcase in the trunk?"

"No," Jones answered as he quickly got in the passenger side. "It's small. I can just hold it in my lap. We're only a couple of minutes from the restaurant. I'm eating at Sea N Suds, by the way, if you're going anywhere in the vicinity."

Jan tried to smile, but it came off as a grimace. She said simply, "In fact, I am going there myself."

"Good! Good!" the old man said enthusiastically. "Then I'm not too much trouble. I'm meeting my best friend there."

Jan grunted a response, then, because she felt as though she had to say something, said, "You're Mr. Jones, aren't you?"

"No 'Mr.,'" he replied. "Just Jones. And you are Jan Hanson; am I right?"

"Yes." Jan nodded as her eyebrows rose. "I am. Have we met?"

"No," Jones laughed, "we haven't. But you are Barry Hanson's wife. And Barry is my best friend."

Jan said nothing as she pulled the car into the parking lot, but she was startled. *What? How could this old man be Barry's best friend? I've never heard Barry mention him in my life. And why on earth did Barry invite someone to lunch with us . . . today of all days!*

Barry was waiting at the corner table when Jan and Jones walked in. Quickly it became obvious that they were *both* coming to the table—together. *What is this?* he wondered. *Another surprise from Jan? She brought someone to lunch? It's that Jones character I've seen around. I cannot believe this. I am not in the mood . . .*

Barry stood as the two approached, but it was an odd greeting each gave and received: a married couple in the throes of divorce, with an old man neither knew, but both thought the other had invited.

They ordered crab claws, oyster sandwiches, and iced tea. Jones seemed happy and relaxed. Jan and Barry, each waiting for the other to explain the old man's presence, made tense small talk until they were interrupted a few minutes later by someone who knew them—and Jones.

When their mutual friend had gone, Barry looked at Jan beside him, Jones across the table, and said, "You know, I don't mean to be rude, but what's going on here?"

"He's *your* best friend," Jan retorted. "You tell me."

"Who's my best friend?"

"Him!" Jan said, indicating Jones.

"What?" Barry said, not certain if he was more confused or angry. "I've never talked to this man in my life."

"Technically, I suppose that's true," Jones said, "but you did wave to me once in the supermarket. And you said hello at church. I've been there several times."

The couple stared incredulously at the old man, not comprehending why he would have deceived them—or whether, in fact, he had.

"All in all, however," Jones continued, "I still maintain that I am the best friend either of you have. There may be people you've known longer than me . . . there may even be lots of people you *like* better than me . . . But today," Jones said with a wise nod of his head, "you don't have a better friend."

Something about this snowy-haired man mesmerized the Hansons, and they sat without speaking as he bit into another crab claw and said, "Most folks figure a true friend is someone who accepts them as they are. But that's dangerous garbage to believe." He gave a dismissive wave of his hand. "The kid who works the drive-through at your local fast-food restaurant accepts you for who you are—because he doesn't care anything about you. But a *true* friend holds you to a higher standard. A true friend brings out the best in you." Jones cocked his head and leaned across the table as if he were about to tell them a secret. "A *best* friend," he said softly, "will tell you the truth . . . and a *wise* best friend will include a healthy dose of perspective."

"And we are supposed to do what?" Barry asked cautiously.

"Just answer a couple of questions," Jones replied, "and listen. You'll be able to decide if it's the truth or not."

Jan and Barry exchanged glances, but before either could speak, Jones said, "Now then. You are having marital problems."

Jan's mouth dropped open. Barry leaned forward, shocked, and asked, "How could you possibly know that?"

"Everyone knows," Jones said.

The Hansons looked stricken. "Everyone!" Barry gasped. "How?"

Jones smiled gently. "Because you're married," he said. "When you're married, those are the kind of problems you have."

Neither Jan nor Barry knew what to say. What the old man had just stated was *so* true that it was rather silly. In fact, Jan couldn't stop herself from smiling back at Jones. "And your point is . . . ?" she prompted.

"Well," Jones said, seemingly barely suppressing a laugh, "I'm not really *to* the point yet, but if I had to make one now, it'd be for you to understand that all people—all lives—are either in a crisis, coming out of a crisis, or headed for a crisis. And marriage can be a natural extension of that. I wanted you to know that things aren't as bad as they seem. Ever! And in this particular situation, you aren't really that different from a billion other married folks. But as usual, you lack perspective."

"You mentioned perspective before," Barry said. "What do you mean?"

Jones looked at the couple thoughtfully for a moment, then without answering Barry, turned to Jan. "Young lady," he began, "was your father a good husband to your mother?"

Jan frowned. "I don't see what that has to do with—"

"Please." Jones held up his hand. "For now, just answer the question. Was your father a good husband to your mother?"

"I think so, yes."

"Did he love her?"

"Yes."

"How did he show your mother he loved her?"

Jan's eyebrows furrowed. "Well . . . ," she began haltingly, "he did things for her."

"What kind of things?" Jones asked.

"You know . . . he washed the dishes occasionally. He fixed things around the house." Then, setting her jaw and cutting a look at Barry, Jan added, "He did things like trimming the shrubbery by the porch, so our house would look nice."

Jones glanced at Barry and did not smile. He was not at all surprised to see that Jan's comment had gone right over her husband's head. "Young lady, how did *this* young man"—he tilted his head toward Barry—"treat *you* when you were dating? I mean, specifically. How did he show he loved you?"

It was as if Jones had turned on a faucet. "Barry was wonderful!" Jan gushed. "He came to my apartment to cook for me—many times. He always helped with the dishes when we ate at home. He fixed things that were broken, just like my dad did for my mom. Once, Barry even went to my parents' house while they were out of town and mowed their lawn! And it wasn't just *those* things; I could tell you a hundred things he used to do." Suddenly her face fell and her lip began to quiver. "But that was when he loved me . . ." Jan began to cry. "He doesn't understand . . ."

Barry had his eyes closed and was quickly shaking his head. "She is absolutely right," he said. "I do *not* understand. And I admit it." Then, opening his eyes and looking squarely at Jones, he said, "But I love her!" Gazing, almost furiously, at Jan, he added, "*I love you.*" But his eyes instantly flitted back to Jones. "I don't know how many more times a day I could tell this woman that I love her or that she's beautiful or that she is great! I gotta tell you, I don't know what to do anymore. This is driving me out of my mind. I didn't sign the papers today, but maybe we *should* get a divorce."

Jan sobbed audibly and hid her face in her hands. Barry looked embarrassed, suddenly realizing that he had been louder than he'd intended, and now a good portion of the restaurant's patrons were glancing nervously toward them. Jones reached across and touched Jan on the shoulder and said quietly to them both, "Let's take a walk."

Both the Hansons were in a daze leaving the restaurant, and neither remembered to pay the check, but a quick smile and a wink from Jones to Nancy at the cash register was all it took to get them out the door quickly.

Within a minute, they were on the beach, walking east. Jan was no longer crying, but she walked with her head down and arms crossed. Barry looked angry again and asked, "What are we doing here? I have to get back to the bank."

Jones continued to walk between the couple and said, "Just a few more minutes. Stay with me for just a bit. Remember," he said as he elbowed the much larger man, "I'm your best friend."

Barry shook his head and rolled his eyes. "This is crazy."

"Young man?" Jones responded, ignoring Barry's irritation, "When you are loved . . . how do you know it?"

"What?" Barry stopped and turned to the old man.

"Keep walking," Jones ordered gently. "Answer the question. When a person loves you—when you have felt loved in the past—how has that person expressed that love?"

"They told me."

"Told you what?"

"That they loved me."

"Be more specific," Jones prodded.

Barry sighed. "A person who loves me tells me what a good job I have done. They tell me that I look nice. They tell me, you know . . . that I am a good man. They tell me they love me."

Jones's eyes narrowed. "Does your wife tell you these things?"

"She used to."

Jan spoke up. "He has so many other people telling him this kind of stuff—he doesn't need to hear it from me."

Jones ignored her comment and continued to address Barry. "If she never tells you she loves you, then how have you known all these years that she does?"

"I just assumed it, I suppose," Barry answered, thinking hard. "I guess I thought she loved me because she never left."

"She's leaving now," Jones stated flatly.

Barry stopped and put his hands on his hips. "Where is this going?"

Jan had stopped as well, so Jones turned to face them both. "One more question," he said seriously. "For you both . . . okay? There has obviously been a lot of water under the bridge—twenty-one years of experiences good and bad. If today you could wave a magic wand, save your marriage, and be happy and secure in your love for each other . . . would you do it?"

Both Barry and Jan, after only a moment's hesitation, but without any sincere hope that it could be accomplished, agreed that, yes, they would save their marriage if it were possible.

"All right, then," Jones said as he smiled and took a deep breath. "Great! Because this is very simple. Your problem is just a matter of perspective."

Barry frowned again and opened his mouth to say something, but Jones wouldn't let him speak. "Nuh-uh-uh," the old man said. "Let *me* talk now. You listen. From both your points of view, all you can see is a failed marriage. But from where I sit, what I see is simply a failure to communicate. Here's what I mean.

"You"—Jones pointed to Jan—"are from America. And you"—he pointed dramatically to Barry—"are from Scotland! Have either of you ever met anyone from Scotland?"

"Yes," Jan said. "I have a cousin who married a guy from Scotland. They live there now."

"Did the man she marry speak English?" Jones asked innocently.

"Of course," Jan answered. "Not that it mattered."

"What do you mean?

"No one could understand him. It was the big family joke one Christmas when they were back in the States."

"Exactly!" Jones exclaimed. "And now you will see my point. A person from America speaks the same English as a person from Scotland, but their dialects are so drastically different that often they can't understand each other at all! And you, my friends, are no different. Your 'language' is exactly the same— you both love each other—but your dialects have gotten in the way.

"Young lady," Jones said gently to Jan, "your husband *does* love you—in fact, I believe he loves you very much. But the dialect he uses to communicate it is *spoken words of approval*. It is also the only dialect he understands. And only by hearing spoken words of approval does *he* ever feel loved."

"I already pointed out how many people *already* tell Barry how wonderful he is," Jan answered defensively.

"That may be true," Jones said with a wry smile, "and there may be hundreds of those . . . but the only person who really counts is *you*. He doesn't love all those other people. He loves *you*. And only *your* words of approval can make him feel loved."

Seeing the understanding beginning to dawn on Jan's face, Jones felt encouraged to continue. "Unfortunately," he said, "the way we *feel* loved is usually the same way we express love. Therefore, your husband did everything he could—over and over again—with the spoken word, to *tell* you how much he loved you. But you never understood, because you have not learned the 'dialect' with which he has tried to communicate that love. You see, the dialect *you* use is one of *favors and deeds*."

Never in their lives—and certainly not in their marriage—had Jan and Barry ever gotten a "lightning bolt," but they knew they were receiving one now. Seeing that he had their undivided attention, Jones plowed on with his explanation. "Young man," he said to Barry, "as desperately as she can, your wife has been trying to convey her love to you by *doing* things for you. She is equally desperate for you to say, 'I love you' by doing things for her! And because you haven't understood *her* dialect, those little favors and deeds didn't seem important to you, and she has felt unloved."

The Hansons stood with their mouths open. Jan had tears in her eyes. "He's right," she said to Barry. "I never understood. I just thought you didn't do those things for me because you didn't love me."

"I didn't understand either," Barry confessed. "I just didn't know those little favors were that important to you."

"Young man," Jones asked, "would it be possible to learn a new dialect in addition to your own? Is it possible for you to wash a few dishes, cook or clean occasionally ... maybe trim that holly bush by the front porch?"

"Yes," Barry answered immediately. "Yes. Absolutely."

"Young lady," Jones said to Jan, "how about you? Are you willing to learn a new dialect too? Can you manage a few spoken words of admiration, a few 'I love yous' here and there?"

"Yes, I can. I will," Jan said, not to Jones, but to Barry, who was visibly moved. She put her arms around him and said, "I am so sorry. I just never knew ..."

"I'm sorry too," Barry said. "And to think we came so close to ... to ending it all."

"And you both loved each other all the time." Jones beamed. "See? You just needed a little perspective."

"You know, sir," Barry said to Jones, still holding Jan tightly, "I *do* love my wife. I would die for her."

Jones chuckled. "That's fine," he said, "but just remember,

she doesn't want you to *die* for her . . . She just wants you to trim that holly bush."

Jan and Barry tried to engage Jones in more conversation, but he was through talking. Politely refusing their offers of any kind of payment—including food or shelter—he excused himself and continued walking east. The Hansons watched him go, more aware than ever that they knew nothing about the old man—not where he was from or if they would see him again.

"Gee . . . the suitcase . . ." Barry murmured as Jones faded into the distance.

"What about it?" Jan asked.

"I should've at least offered to carry it."

Chapter 3

THE SUN WAS SHINING BRIGHTLY AS JONES AMBLED UP
onto the Gulf State Park Pier, where I had been waiting. I was
sitting on a picnic table, my feet on the bench, nursing a soft
drink and watching the fishermen.

We greeted each other again and began to talk—mostly
about me and my life since he left. It wasn't so much that I
wanted only to talk about me, but he was still reticent to discuss
himself. "Here and there" was the answer to where he had been.
"A lot of things" was the response to what he had been doing. In
a way, it was frustrating, but I knew better than to push any
more than I already had.

He declined my invitation to stay at our house, though he
congratulated me on *having* one. Jones pointed underneath the
pier and, affecting a serious tone, asked, "It *is* nicer than your

first place, right?" Then Jones told me about Jan and Barry. He wasn't breaking a confidence, he explained, because he was only telling his own part of the story anyway. "And besides," he added, "they'll be telling everyone what they've learned soon enough."

As he laid out the idea behind love expressed in different dialects, I asked if there were more than just the two he had revealed to the Hansons. "Yes," Jones answered. "There seem to be four major dialects that we use to convey and feel loved. There are combinations and subgroups, too, I suppose, but basically four."

"Okay," I prompted, "I know about spoken words of approval, and favors and deeds. What are the others?"

"The third dialect," Jones began, "is one of physical contact. This can be from a simple pat on the back all the way to the other end of the spectrum, a sexual relationship. A quick back rub, a head scratch, a hug or a kiss—these are all common forms of this dialect. People who speak the dialect of physical contact tend to feel most loved when affection is expressed in this form. Sometimes that's the *only* way they feel loved."

"And that is how they show their love as well?" I asked.

"Absolutely," Jones said. "It's not right or wrong. It's just the only dialect they understand. So, for the sake of conversation, consider the person who speaks physical contact to be like a cat."

I raised my eyebrows. "Excuse me?"

"Cats are almost exclusively creatures of physical contact," Jones answered, himself grinning like the Cheshire cat. "You don't really have to feed them—you know cats . . . if a cat's hungry, he'll kill something. Cats don't pay any attention to what you say or do. No reason to call one. He wouldn't come if you did. Cats just want to be rubbed and scratched. That is how they feel love. And how does a cat *express* love? A cat will rub against you with its face or back. 'Touch me,' a cat is saying. Some people are the same way."

"That is so true!" I exclaimed. "Amazing. And what about the fourth dialect?"

"Number four would be love expressed in quality time," Jones said. "To a person who speaks this dialect, it doesn't matter if you touch them, do something for them, or tell them repeatedly that you love them. The only thing that matters is quality time together.

"Now, you're not a 'quality time' person, Andy," Jones said with a laugh, "but let me ask you something. Has your wife ever said something like, 'I wish we spent more time together,' or 'You're just not around that much'?"

I nodded uncertainly, beginning to suspect his conclusion, and answered, "As a matter of fact, yes, she does. And you know, I work at home, so I always thought, *What do you mean I'm not around? How could we spend more time together? Holy cow! I'm here all day long!*"

"Yes, you are there all day long," Jones avowed, "but not with *her.* Your wife speaks the dialect of quality time. She craves time alone with only you. That is how she expresses her love. And for you to have a wife who is happy and who feels secure in your love, you *must* learn to speak this dialect. It is expressed by giving her periods of undivided attention, listening to the details of her day, her dreams and concerns."

"To be honest, I feel kind of ridiculous that I never knew this," I confessed.

"Don't," Jones said with a wave of his hand. "Why would you know it? We grow up expecting everyone else to be just like us. And they aren't. But now that you know . . ."

"Yes, now that I know, I can do something about it." I paused, trying to take it all in, then had a thought. "Hey, Jones, you said that physical-touch people were like cats . . ." I grinned mischievously. "Is there an animal that you use to represent quality time?"

The old man ducked his head, sheepishly. "Yes, son, I do. I have always likened a person who receives and expresses love by quality time to a canary. A canary says, 'Just be with me!' A canary never really notices who gives it food or water. It doesn't care what you say to it and certainly does not need to be touched. A canary is happiest when you sit and listen carefully to its song. And a canary that is ignored will die. Not from lack of food, but from a lack of love and attention."

"What am I, Jones?" I asked then, studying his face.

"You, my friend," Jones said with amusement, "are a puppy dog. You, I am quite sure, feel loved by spoken words of approval."

"That is exactly right!" I laughed. "But why a puppy dog?"

"Well, think about it," Jones said. "Tell a puppy how wonderful he is and his *whole body* wags. And how do you teach a puppy most effectively? With praise! 'Good boy!' 'There's a good dog-gie!' But here's a word of caution to those who love a puppy dog, or a person who speaks the dialect of spoken words of approval. Nothing—and I mean nothing—is more devastating than words of *dis*approval spoken in an angry tone of voice. Puppies cower as if they are under attack. And so do people who express and receive love in this dialect."

"Okay, we have cats, canaries, and puppy dogs . . ." I was counting them off on my fingers. "What is the animal for favors and deeds? That's a person like Jan, right?"

"Right," Jones said. "Jan—and people like her—are goldfish."

I laughed out loud. "I'm sure she'll be glad to hear that," I said.

"And I'm sure you're gonna tell her!" he fired back at me with a twinkle in his eye.

"Jones," I responded, still laughing, "I'm gonna tell everybody."

He shrugged. "Well, it might not be a bad thing for folks to know. It isn't just married couples that can make use of this knowledge. These dialects, when you get good at spotting them, can help you communicate with your kids, your friends, even people you work with. Yep, no matter the age or relationship, everybody—every single body—speaks a dialect. Won't the world be a better place when we understand them all?"

I thought about that for a moment, then remembered . . . "Jones, why is Jan a goldfish?"

"A goldfish feels loved based purely on favors and deeds. You can't really touch them. I don't know if they can hear you, even if you do talk to them, so they don't want your affirmation. And as far as quality time, they don't care if you're there or not! A goldfish just wants you to feed them and clean the bowl. And, oh yeah, straighten the castle while you're there!"

I hooted in laughter. "You really have it nailed, Jones."

"Well," he said modestly, "it's just something I noticed over the years. Just a little different perspective on how we relate to one another." He stood, stretched, and remarked, "Getting to be late afternoon. 'Bout time, I'm sure, for you to go home and spend a little quality time with that pretty wife of yours."

I stood, too, ready to go, but then was suddenly uneasy. It occurred to me just how much I owed this old man—a person about whom I knew virtually nothing. And yet somehow, I loved him. And I knew he loved me.

"Jones," I started, "are you sure you won't come home—"

"Hey, I appreciate it. I really do," he said, "but I'm fine. I'm not hungry, cold, or wet. Don't you worry about old Jones. Actually, I have another appointment. So, scat, okay?" And he smiled at me, picked up his suitcase, and walked me off the pier.

At my car, I asked, "Will I see you again? While you're here, I mean?"

"Oh yeah!" he answered. "And I'll be here for a while. Be looking for me." Then he swept his hands over his T-shirt and jeans. "I'll be the one wearing this!"

Chapter 4

JONES CROSSED THE BEACH ROAD AND BEGAN TO WALK through the state park. Within an hour, darkness had begun to fall, and the rich reds and purples of the evening sky created a compelling stage for the night sounds. Traversing the park's first tiny bridge, the old man listened to the frogs and crickets singing in the brackish swamp. Then he heard a soft rush of air overhead and looked up to see an owl beginning its evening hunt. Slowing, as if he recognized the area, Jones heard the splash of what he imagined to be a large fish—or a small alligator.

He stopped beside an old pine and placed his battered suitcase on its side, sat down on it, and leaned his back against the base of the tree. Traffic was light on the road. It was used mostly by locals as a shortcut to reach Highway 59. Tourists rarely ventured this way.

Jones wasn't tired. Still, he closed his eyes . . .

WALKER MILES RARELY TOOK THIS ROUTE AND WOULDN'T have done so this evening had the traffic light on the beach road not been red. It was a long light, he knew, so to avoid the wait, he made a right turn into the park.

As he drove the tightly curved road in his midsized sedan, Walker thought about his life. He was a pharmaceutical sales rep, fifty-three years old and single—again—having divorced for the second time only four months earlier. He had moved to the beach in hopes of a new start. His vacations in the past had been enjoyable in this area, Walker had reasoned, so his intention was to live where there seemed at least a chance for happiness. After all, a *chance* for happiness was all he could hope for any-more. At least, that's how he felt. Always. For Walker, happi-ness was an elusive, moving target that seemed to perpetually flit just beyond his grasp. His thoughts were consumed by possibilities of problems and mistakes, personal slights and professional sabotage. Lately, he had even been contemplating suicide.

Walker's first wife, Kendra, had left, explaining that she could no longer live with a man whose emotional role model was the donkey Eeyore from *Winnie-the-Pooh*. His second wife, Debra, on her way out, had alluded to another character from a children's book: "Walker," she had said sadly, "the sky is *not* always falling. I hope one day you will realize that."

But tonight, he was depressed—a familiar state for him—and tired.

As Walker's headlights came on, he drove over the park's first bridge and saw a figure just past it, sitting several yards off the road. *Bum. Drifter. Old. Really old.* The thoughts that ran through Walker's mind as he glanced at the man were not flattering. He was certainly not inclined to slow down, much less *stop*—so when he did, Walker muttered to himself, "What *are* you doing?"

For a moment, Walker just sat there, in the middle of the road. Then, with a sigh, he shook his head, checked the rearview mirror, and slowly backed up, mumbling, "I am an idiot." When the car paralleled the old man, Walker rolled down the passenger window and peered cautiously into the semidarkness.

The old man lifted a hand in greeting. "How do you do?" he called.

"Do you need help?" Walker asked in response. The old man did not answer, but stood, picked up whatever he'd been sitting on, and eased over to the car.

As the man approached, Walker rolled the window almost to the top. Every fiber of his being was screaming at him to drive away, leave this place, and get away from this creepy situation; but for some reason, he did not move.

"I'm sorry," the old man said kindly as he stopped beside Walker's car. "Did you ask me a question? I don't hear quite as well as I used to."

"Uh . . . well . . . ," Walker faltered as he looked up at the old man, whose white hair and blue eyes stood out in stark relief to the muted colors in the faded light around him.

"Say again . . . ?" the old man prompted.

"Well," Walker said, "I was just wondering if you needed help."

"Whew!" the old man sighed, shaking his head as if in wonder. "Don't we all! Don't we all!"

"I beg your pard—"

"Oh, young man, you don't have to beg," the old man interrupted. "I'll ride with you." And with that, he opened the door and got in—him and his suitcase—before Walker could protest.

Shocked, Walker didn't know whether to be angry and demand that the intruder leave, or get out of the car himself. And he was certain—or thought he was certain—that he had locked the car door.

But before Walker could utter a word, his uninvited guest held out his hand. "Jones," he said simply. "No 'Mr.' to it." Then, opening his eyes widely as if seeing the younger man clearly for the first time, he added, "Say . . . you're Walker Miles. I'm sorry I didn't recognize you."

Frowning, Walker said, "Am I supposed to . . . uh . . . do I know you?"

"Noooo," Jones said. "I saw you in Dr. Surek's office a week ago. You wouldn't remember me, but I heard him say your name a time or two. I don't forget a name. Or a face it looks like."

Walker was still leery. He called on all the doctors in the area—Chris Surek included—but he rarely paid attention to any of their patients. Was this man sick? he wondered. "You said you needed help?" Walker prompted.

Jones blinked innocently. "Did I? Oh. Well, how about a ride to Foley? You're going that way, right?"

Walker eased off the brake and turned the overhead light off at the same time, keeping an eye on the strange old man next to him. "Yeah, I'm going to Foley," he said as he began to speed up. "Any particular place you want to be dropped off?"

"No. I don't think I am particularly particular tonight." Jones chuckled at his word choice, then saw that the younger man had not joined him with even a smile. He tried another tack. "I was in a city one night—Chicago, it was, come to think of it—and I saw a man chase a hat that had blown off someone's head into the street. A car hit him and killed him dead."

Walker glanced at the old man, disgusted, and said, "Why on earth would you tell me that?"

"I just think it's amazing," Jones answered, looking straight ahead, "that a person could lose everything, chasing nothing."

Neither spoke for a moment. The car's headlights wound through the park, dancing off the blacktop and flaring among the trees. Walker drove as if he were concentrating on where he was going, but inside, he was merely being haunted by where he had already been. He flexed his fingers on the steering wheel and finally answered with a sigh, "Well, that's me."

Jones shifted in the seat and clucked his tongue. "Yeah, that's everybody one time or another. But why do you say it's you?"

Walker's mind raced. He was intelligent, sane, and from a good family. He could not rationally come up with one single reason why he had stopped for this old man in the first place. Now he was about to reveal his most private thoughts—and he did *not* want to. But strangely, it was as if Walker were watching someone else have the conversation. Logic warned him to keep quiet, but something more powerful gave him a sense of well-being, of trust. He relaxed and began to talk to Jones as if he'd known him for years.

Walker told him about growing up—about being the youngest of three kids, and about the pain of his father's alcoholism. He talked about his own marriages, the many jobs he had held, most successful for a time, but ultimately ending because of his own inability to be happy. And on and on he went, baring his soul as if to an old friend.

BY THE TIME WALKER HAD TOLD JONES EVERYTHING there was to tell, they were on their fourth refill of coffee at Waffle House. Once again, Walker was still overcome with amazement that he was here at all, talking to this old-timer, but he admitted to himself that it was as if he had found a long-lost friend.

"To a degree," Walker said, "I suppose I always felt like a loser because my dad was an alcoholic."

"Well," Jones answered innocently, "maybe your dad was an alcoholic because you were a loser." Then he laughed and held up his hands as if to fend off Walker's blows. "Just kidding. *Juuuust* kidding."

Walker wasn't certain whether he should be offended or not.

"Look, young man," Jones went on, a bit more seriously, "your father and all his problems are in the past. Here he is, *dead*, and you're still dragging this 'my dad was an alcoholic' thing around! It's time to stop letting your history control your destiny."

"I know, I know," Walker said, his eyes closed now. "I know this. I know I shouldn't think so much about the past. I know I shouldn't worry. I know I have nothing to be depressed about . . ." He opened his eyes and looked at Jones with all the frustration of fifty-three years boiling over. Then, trying to speak quietly though he felt like screaming, Walker said, "I really *am* aware. I just . . . can't stop. These feelings have ruined my life." He paused, and then, in a broken whisper, said, "I don't know what to do."

Jones reached out, took Walker by the forearm, and squeezed gently. Walker instantly relaxed and began to breathe deeply. "Look into my eyes, son," the old man said then, and Walker did.

"There isn't any drastic action you need to be taking because you feel this way," the old man said. "Like all things that seem a big deal . . . this *ain't* a big deal. Okay?"

Walker nodded.

Jones seemed to relax a bit. Then he took a deep breath and announced, "There are two things you need to know about how you feel, and one thing you need to do. The first thing you need to know is that you worry—or you feel this crazy fear—because you're smart."

Walker's face fell, and he sat back in the booth. "Hang on, now," the old man softly scolded, as if he had read Walker's mind. "I'm not being condescending. I'm not trying to shine you on. This is *truth* . . . just a little different perspective. You are a logical young man. So sit still. You'll appreciate this."

Jones smiled, took a sip of his coffee, and started again. "You worry," he said, "because you're smart—like I said." The old man looked around as if to keep a secret, then added, "The dumber folks among us don't worry much. They ain't afraid of nothing." Walker's brow furrowed in confusion, so Jones explained: "Here it is, young man: smart people are generally more creative and imaginative than dumb people. You agree, right?"

Walker still had no idea where the old man was going. "I suppose," he said.

"Well, that's why smart people get tripped up with worry and fear. Worry . . . fear . . . is just a misuse of the creative imagination that has been placed in each of us. Because we are smart and creative, we imagine all the things that *could* happen, that *might* happen, that *will* happen if this or that happens. See what I mean?"

Walker had begun to nod attentively, and the beginning of a smile was emerging on his face. "That's me," he said. "Not the smart part . . ."

Jones waved him off. "I know what you mean. Anyway . . . ,"

he continued, "dumb people, on the other hand, don't worry about anything! They aren't afraid of anything! You've seen the TV shows. The only thing crazier than the guy that says, 'Watch this!' is the guy that says, 'Heck, I can do that!'"

Walker laughed out loud with the old man. "I guess you're right," he said.

"Sure, I'm right," Jones replied. "Smart people—like you—consistently misuse the creative imagination that has been placed inside them to scream, 'Fire!' where there isn't even any smoke."

"So how do I turn that part of me off?" Walker asked. "It is a problem. I *do* worry about things that logically should not even be in my head."

"If you know that *logically* these doubts and fears should not even be in your head, then the easiest way to defeat them . . . is with logic."

Walker stared intently, but shook his head. "I don't understand."

"You will," Jones replied. "So those are the two things you need to know: one, that you think the way you do because you're smart; and two, you have to defeat those thoughts with logic."

Jones shifted in the booth, put both elbows on the table, and, concentrating hard on the man in front of him, said, "When doubts and fears assail us, we subconsciously calculate the possibilities. 'This might *really* happen!' we tell ourselves, or 'What will happen *if* . . . ?'" He leaned a little closer. "And soon, we are so paralyzed by the idea that disaster is imminent that we cannot function in our work—and even our relationships dissolve. We have imagined our way to self-destruction. And that's what has happened to you, my friend. What you must do—to defeat bad logic with good—is to deflect your subconscious from calculating possibilities. Instead, direct your mind to calculate the *odds*. You can learn very quickly to calculate the odds of an event occurring and eliminate it as even a remote possibility in your life." Then, borrowing a pen from a passing waitress, Jones said, "Consider what I am about to give you to be an authoritative estimate on the things you worry about." Reaching for his napkin, he wrote down "40%." Then he raised his eyes to Walker. "Forty percent," he said. "Forty percent of the things you worry about will never occur anyway."

Returning his gaze to the napkin, Jones next wrote, "30%." "Thirty percent," he said, looking up again, "of the things you worry about are things that have already happened—in the past. And all the worry in the world ain't gonna change what's *already* happened, right?"

Walker nodded in agreement.

Jones wrote, "12%" on the napkin. "I'm thinking twelve percent of all worries have to do with needless imaginings about our health. *My leg hurts. Do I have cancer? My head hurts. Do I have a tumor? My daddy died of a heart attack when he was sixty, and I'm fifty-nine.*" Jones looked up. "You get me?"

"I do."

"Ten percent," he said next, as he wrote, "would be petty-little-nothing worries about what other people think." He looked up. "And we can't do nothin' about what other people think."

Walker tilted his head to read the napkin that was upside down in front of him. "So if my math is right," he said, "that leaves eight percent." He looked at Jones. "Eight percent for what?"

"Eight percent," Jones answered, "for legitimate concerns." He held up a finger. "But . . . it should be noted that these legitimate concerns are things that can actually be dealt with. Most people spend so much time fearing the things that are never going to happen or can't be controlled that they have no energy to deal with the few things they can actually handle."

"That's me," Walker said simply.

"Not anymore," Jones answered. "Now, tell me: what are the immediate thoughts in your mind, say, during the first ten minutes after you wake up every morning?"

Walker shrugged. "You know . . . what I have to do, who I have to call, the things I need to deal with first, I guess."

"These would be your most pressing challenges of the day?"

"Yes. Absolutely."

"Okay," Jones began, "I'm not saying that you *don't* think about the things you have to do . . . but I want you to mix in some other thoughts as well. Leave a pad and pen beside your bed, and when you wake up, grab it and take it everywhere with you for the first ten or so minutes of your morning. On that pad, I want you to list things in your life that you are grateful for. You can list names, objects, feelings . . . anything. Remember to list clean sheets and a roof over your head—knowing there are millions who spent the night without either. As you eat breakfast or skip it, remember the millions who have none. Be generous and creative as you list the many things you have to be grateful for, young man. Don't be shy about writing the same ones down every day. And *write* them down. Thinking about this will not do the trick." Jones smiled widely. "But then, you already know that. After all, it is your own imagination with which you are doing battle!"

Jones leaned back now and set down his pen with a finality that said he was drawing their time to a close. "You will feel differently from now on," Jones said leaning back. "Many people who worry too much say that they cannot focus—that it costs them their jobs and relationships. That is incorrect. A person consumed by worry *can* focus. Isn't it obvious? Worry *is* focus! But it is focus on the wrong things. Young man," Jones said to Walker, "you are now equipped to calculate the odds. From this point forward, you will focus on what can be controlled. And you will no longer be sad or worried. You will be grateful! After all, the seeds of depression cannot take root in a grateful heart.

"Now, wash up," Jones ordered, pointing Walker out of the booth and to the restroom.

Walker stood and gazed awkwardly at Jones for a moment. Then he placed his hand on the old man's shoulder. "Thank you, Jones," he said solemnly. "You know, if I hadn't run into you tonight, I might've—"

"Go," Jones said gently, clapping his palm over the hand on his shoulder. "I know. And you're welcome."

Less than two minutes later, Walker came out of the rest-room to find the check paid and the old man gone.

Chapter 5

"Do you know Jones?" Robert Craft asked me as we stood on the clubhouse steps. Robert was the owner of Craft Farms, one of the nicest golf clubs on the Gulf Coast, and the place I had come on this day for lunch.

"Yes, I do," I answered, glancing down the length of the building, where Jones stood, foot on his suitcase, surrounded by young people. Guys and girls, most appeared to be in their late teens or early twenties. They were laughing, hanging on the old man's every word. "Who are the kids?"

"Bag attendants, waitstaff, greens maintenance . . . You're looking at all the young people who work here who aren't supposed to be doing something else right now." Robert grinned and added, "And probably a few who *are* supposed to be doing something else."

"How do you know Jones?" I asked Robert.

"Daddy knew him," he answered, still looking at the gaggle of youth surrounding the old man. "Before Daddy ever met Mama, Jones helped him out of some jam." Robert turned to me. "It wasn't a big deal, you know. One of those 'here's another way of looking at it' kind of things, but Daddy never forgot it—or him."

"Do you see him often?" I asked.

Robert got a strange look on his face. "Do *you*?" he came back.

"I asked first," I said, and we both laughed.

Looking back toward the old man, Robert said, "I asked Daddy one time what Jones looked like when he was younger. Daddy said he looked just like that." Robert jerked a thumb in Jones's direction. Then, remembering my question, he added, "I guess I've seen him . . . oh, ten or twelve different periods in my life."

"What do you mean, 'periods'?"

"You know . . . he stays around for a while; then he's gone for a while . . . like that." He snapped his fingers. "Sometimes, he's gone so long that I forget about him. But he always comes back."

Robert gazed out across the eighteenth fairway. "Daddy started this, you know," he said, with a broad sweep of his arm across the landscape. "It was all gladiola fields before it was a golf course. When I took over several years ago, Daddy told me to let the old man have run of the place."

"Really?"

"Mm-hmm. He doesn't play golf. Just hangs around and talks to people. I'll see him sometimes in the dining room or out by the putting green—in some serious conversation with someone or another. I don't know where he sleeps. Or for that matter, *if* he sleeps. He never sleeps around here.

"We try to comp his meals," Robert continued, "but he always pays. Big tipper, too, the waitstaff says. I don't know where he gets the money, but I guess he keeps it in that suitcase. God knows, there can't be any clothes in there . . . he always wears the same thing."

Another burst of laughter erupted from the group surrounding the old man. Robert smiled and shook his head. "They love him."

Curious, I asked, "Do you mind him being here? He doesn't *look* the country club type, you know." Then I motioned toward Robert's employees. "Is he taking up too much of their time?"

"I've got to tell you," Robert said, "if I could figure a way to make the old man *stay* here, I would. These kids walk on air after they talk with him. They're better. They're sharper—in every way. My son—you know Mitch—tells me he gives them advice—just little things, mind you—but they listen, and the old man's advice works." He shook his head in wonder. "When have you ever seen a bunch of kids interested in an eccentric old guy like that?" Then he added, "And have you heard the talk around town? It isn't just the kids. People are, like, looking him up or something, seeking him out. And you know Jones; he'll talk to anybody." Robert paused, thinking. "He's been around longer this time, I think," he said finally.

Jones had looked our way, spotted us, waved and continued talking with the young people. I shook my head in wonder, too, and softly, only loud enough for Robert to hear, said, "Jones."

"Not *Mr.* Jones," Robert responded jokingly.

"Oh, no," I said with a snicker. "Just Jones."

As I reached out to give Robert a parting handshake, he said, "You know, Daddy didn't call him Jones."

"Really?" I said. "What did he call him?"

"Well, Daddy met him when he came through with the migrant workers—picking the gladiolas—and Daddy called him what *they* did, what they still do. They call him Garcia."

JONES HAD ALREADY SAID GOOD-BYE TO MOST OF THE kids, who had either drifted to their cars in the parking lot or back to work. But as he moved toward the shade of the club-house porch overlooking the lake, he noticed three of the young people hadn't left.

"Where're you going, Jones?" asked Caroline, the tall girl beside him. "You want a Coke?" she said. "You guys?" she asked the others, then without waiting for an answer, said, "Four Cokes," and headed for the clubhouse.

Caroline had long, red hair. She was taller than Jones, pretty in a casual sort of way, a high school senior, and one of the most popular kids in the area. Caroline's father was a mortgage banker;

her mother, active in community affairs—the family seemed to have it all together.

As he walked toward the porch, Jones glanced at Amelia, Caroline's best friend, who was walking alongside him. Amelia, a sophomore in college and home on spring break, was two years older than Caroline. Amelia was a liberal arts major whose family history was, as she put it, "cloudy." Next to Amelia was Ritchie Weber, a handsome seventeen-year-old.

The small group stepped up onto the porch and walked around back, away from the entrance. Jones eased himself into one of the white rocking chairs, as did Amelia beside him. Caroline approached shortly, distributed the soft drinks, and sat on the porch's wooden floor. Ritchie perched on the rail, with his back to the lake.

"What do you want to talk about, Jones?" Ritchie said. The young man's dark, mocha-colored skin gleamed in the early afternoon sun, and his clear face and straight teeth made him look like an actor or model. Extremely sharp-witted, Ritchie put his efforts into academics, eschewing the usual sports (except golf). With his high GPA, he had already been assured a full scholarship in the fall.

"Me?" Jones answered Ritchie, with a false innocence. "I didn't want to talk about anything. I was coming over here to take a nap!"

"Come on!" Caroline teased, bumping the old man with the pink flip-flop on her foot. "You know you want us here. You love us. So . . . talk, Jones!"

The old man chuckled and took a sip of his drink. "Okay, let's talk. But you start. Young man," Jones raised his styrofoam cup to Ritchie, "you first. Ask a question."

"Okay," said Ritchie, eagerly, "here ya go: how do you keep a marriage from ending in divorce?"

Jones feigned surprise. "Wow!" he said. "Nothing easy from you! How about, 'What'll the Cubs do this year?' or 'When will the trout start biting?'"

Ritchie just waited expectantly.

"That's your subject?" Jones asked finally. "Are you sure?"

"I'm sure," Ritchie said.

Jones took a deep breath and blew it out. "Okay . . . are you married?"

The two girls tittered.

"Jones!" Ritchie all but shouted. "You know I'm not married."

"He's got some girlfriends, though," Caroline teased.

"If you aren't married," Jones asked without any hint of guile, "then why do you care about how you keep a marriage from ending in divorce?"

Ritchie shrugged. "My parents are about the only ones I know who are married to their original—"

"Mine too," Caroline interrupted.

"Okay," Ritchie corrected, "then mine and yours. Anyway, lots of guys and girls are getting married pretty young . . . people we know." He looked at his two companions for agreement, and they nodded. "But it seems like they all get divorced after a few years," he went on. "So, long story short, the reason I'm asking how to keep a marriage from ending in divorce is that there *has* to be something you can learn while you are dating! I mean, I hope there is!"

"You are a wise young man," Jones said, his chair rocking slowly. "It's obvious you kids are smart—school and good teachers will do that for you—but wisdom is something altogether different. Wisdom can be gathered in your downtime. Wisdom that can change the very course of your life will come from the people you are around, the books you read, and the things you listen to or watch on radio or television.

"Of course, bad information is gathered in your downtime too. Bad information that can change the very course of your life will come from the people you are around, the books you read, and the things you listen to or watch on radio or television."

Ritchie, Caroline, and Amelia listened carefully. They had been around Jones long enough to know that he rarely answered a question directly. There was always some greater envelope around the nugget of truth he dispensed.

"One of wisdom's greatest benefits," Jones continued, "is accurate discernment—the learned ability to immediately tell right from wrong. Good from evil. Acceptable from unacceptable. Time well spent from time wasted. The right decision from the wrong decision. And many times this is simply a matter of having the correct perspective."

"Okay, Jones," Ritchie said, "we knew you'd get around to your favorite word eventually, but how does perspective relate to wisdom?"

"Here's the connection," Jones said. "One way to define wisdom is *the ability to see, into the future, the consequences of your choices in the present.* That ability can give you a completely different perspective on what the future might look like.

"Here's how it works in its highest earthly form. Wisdom will allow a person to split the hair of choice so accurately that most men would say it is impossible." Jones spoke in a low tone so that the young people had to lean toward him to hear. "So listen to me now—pinpoint accuracy in choices of all kinds *is* a possibility for you! You see, with a degree of intelligence and a hint of wisdom, most people can tell the difference between good and bad. However, it takes a truly *wise* person to discern that oh-so-thin line between good and best. And *that* line, my friends, is the line that separates a roll of the dice about your future, from a sure thing . . . from trying, as the Bible says, to 'see through a dark glass' and having a perspective that allows you to see clearly the long-term consequences of your choices. How does all this relate to choosing a partner for life? Just the difference between a marriage made on earth from a marriage made in heaven."

"Jones, no offense," Amelia said, "but what does this have to do with Ritchie's question . . . that I can barely remember anymore?"

They all laughed, Jones included. "No offense taken. All right," he said. "Most folks think marriage is about commitment—and it is—but the committin' is a whole heck of a lot easier if you've made a wise choice to begin with. That's why I know the young man here"—Jones indicated Ritchie—"is gonna have a better marriage than most folks. Why? Because he is already seeking and gathering wisdom that will help him make the perfect choice.

"Now . . . ," Jones turned his gaze to the ceiling fan above them and said, "let's excavate this situation a little more before we sift through the dirt to see where we are." He looked at Amelia. "Young lady, why do folks get married?"

Amelia instantly reddened and wondered if she was being tested. She opened her mouth, then clamped it shut.

"It ain't a trick question," Jones prompted. "Just why?"

"Okay . . . because they love each other?"

"Is that all?"

Amelia laughed. "I don't know what you want me to say!"

"No wrong answers," Jones said. "We are just excavating here. So, because they love each other. And . . . ?"

"Because they love each other and they want to spend the rest of their lives together," Amelia said in a rush.

Jones turned to Caroline. "And how do you know you love someone enough to get married?" he asked her.

"Well . . ." Caroline began tentatively, "that person is the only person you want to be around. You think about them constantly. You want to hold them—"

"You want to 'do it' with them," Ritchie cut in, his eyebrows waggling. Caroline gave him a dirty look.

"That was such a 'guy' thing to say, Ritchie," Amelia said scornfully.

"Yeah, well," he responded, not the least bit contrite, "I'm a guy. There you go."

"Okay, okay," Jones interrupted with a chuckle. "Actually, that's part of it, right? The physical attraction?" Three heads bobbed affirmatively. "But how do you know you love someone enough to spend the *rest of your life* together?"

Jones looked from one young person to the other. None spoke.

Finally, Caroline said, "I never really thought of that . . ."

"Nobody else gives much thought to it either," Jones answered, his face sad.

For a moment the three friends sat in silence, digesting what they thought the old man had just told them. Then Ritchie spoke up. "Jones, are you saying that now, while we are dating— while we are young—we should be thinking about who we want to spend the rest of our lives with?"

"I don't know," Jones answered. "What do you think? The alternative is that you spend your young years dating . . . and *not* thinking about who you want to spend the rest of your life with. Does that seem wise to you?"

Silence.

Jones let them stew a bit, then said, "Think with old Jones, now . . . Here's what happens in most of those marriages you asked about earlier. And I want to make myself clear: I'm not talking about what we can do to make an existing marriage better—and we're not covering every base here. I'm telling you one aspect of what happens in normal marriages every day: a young man and a young woman spot each other across a crowded room, and sparks fly."

Caroline giggled.

"Shhh!" Ritchie scolded. "Go on, Jones."

"They meet and soon are 'in love.' They can't bear to be apart. Every moment they are apart is spent thinking about the other." Jones spoke dramatically, batting his eyelashes for effect. "And when they are together, it is all the two can do to keep their hands off each other. If they could kiss day and night, they would!"

"Okay, we get it," Amelia said. "They're in love."

"Yes," Jones agreed, "they are. In fact, they are so in love that each has become more important to the other than anything else in their lives. You see, the girl has a passion for horses. All her life, she has ridden horses, read horse magazines, dreamed of the horses she would own . . . but the young man is allergic to horses. He can't be around them and wouldn't if he could. They're huge, and they scare him. But that gal of his loves him so much that quietly, with no one even aware of her thought process, she decides, *He is much more important to me than horses! I don't necessarily need horses in my life* . . . and she chooses her young man—her love.

"Now, the young man is just as crazy about her as she is him. He *loooooooves* her," Jones said, pooching his lips as he said the word *love*, eliciting giggles from his young friends. "But the thing about him," Jones continued, "is that he grew up fishing. Since he was a little boy, this young man has fished with his family. Fishing and football. Nothing like it. If he wasn't fishing, he was watching football."

"And I'll bet she hates to fish," Ritchie said.

"Can't stand it!" Jones concurred. "She isn't really a 'water' person. Doesn't like to eat fish either. And"—Jones affected a look of horror—"she thinks football is stupid."

"Here we go . . ." Amelia began.

"No, no," Jones said. "Everything is all right, because he loves her so much. He is willing to do anything, sacrifice anything, just so he can spend the rest of his life with her. So . . . quietly, with no one even aware that he is doing so, the young man makes a decision: *She is so much more important to me than fishing,* he tells himself. *I don't need to fish. Why do I need to fish when I have her? And football? Well, I like it . . . but it's not nearly as important as her.*"

Jones spread his hands. "And there you have it," he said.

"There we have what?" Ritchie asked. "What? What do they do?"

"They get married, of course," Jones laughed. "And that is your answer to why so many marriages end in divorce!"

The three young people looked confusedly at one another. Clearly, they all decided, none of them had any idea what point the old man was trying to make. "Jones," Amelia said slowly, "we don't get it. What happened? Why would their marriage end in divorce? Isn't that what everybody does? Compromise? Aren't there just some things you . . . well . . . live with? Like whether they squeeze the toothpaste tube from the bottom or the middle?"

Jones smiled and patted Amelia's hand. Then he stood up and motioned for Ritchie to take his chair. Leaning against the porch rail, with his back to the lake so he could see all three young people at once, the old man smiled gently and said, "Yes, if it was as simple as the toothpaste tube, there probably wouldn't be any problems. See . . . these two fell hard for each other and let a physical attraction trump everything else in its way. Don't get me wrong; I'm not saying physical attraction is not important—it is. But you can be physically attracted to a lot of people. You don't believe me? Turn on the TV or walk down the beach.

"Here's my point. Somewhere along the line, there has to be something to share when the physical attraction is not on your mind twenty-four hours a day, because here's what happens: after three months or three years—*sometime*, you can be sure— the physical thing won't be the absolute, number-one, most important thing in that couple's life. There will be some other things that begin to be important too. Now, a lot of young ladies at this point begin to think, *Gosh! Am I going to spend the rest of my entire life never riding a horse?* And young men start thinking, *Holy cow! Am I really willing to live the rest of my life not fishing? Can I never watch football ever again? In my* life?"

Caroline, Amelia, and Ritchie remained quiet. They understood, but Jones hammered the point home. "Pretty soon," he concluded, "that guy at the office, with horse pictures on his wall, is a comforting ear to the young lady. The waitress at the restaurant, the cute one who always knows the football scores, she understands the young man's problems . . . Nobody meant for it to happen, but remember, you can be attracted to a lot of people."

"That's a pretty sad picture, Jones," Amelia said. "Gee . . ."

"Happens every day," the old man said with a sigh. "Doesn't have to happen to you, though."

"How can we avoid it?" Caroline asked.

"Well, hey," Ritchie said, "that's fairly obvious, isn't it? I mean, just be careful not to fall in love or lust or whatever with someone you don't want to hang with."

"Yeah, but I don't think it's that simple," Amelia said. "Remember, Jones said that the guy and the girl decided *quietly* that they would compromise, without anyone even knowing they were doing so. And there is also the fact that we hide our true selves sometimes. What if my guy never told me he didn't like horses?"

Again, they all looked at Jones. He shrugged and said, "Well, of course, one is always susceptible to a skillful liar, but barring that, there is a wonderful filter most of us possess that allows us to determine if a young man or woman is suitable as a potential life partner."

"What filter?" Caroline asked.

"Your friends," Jones said simply. "Your family, too, for sure, but nothing filters the true person like friends."

"Explain," Ritchie requested.

"Curiously, it usually works in the reverse from what most of us expect. For instance, young man," Jones said to Ritchie, "you probably thought that I meant your friends should pass judgment on your young lady. Is that correct?"

Ritchie looked at the two girls, whose faces indicated that this is what they had assumed as well. "Uh ... yes. That's what I thought you meant."

"No!" Jones said. "What you are interested in is whether or not *she* likes your friends! Now, assuming that you hang with good people, wise friends, does she encourage your participation in activities with your friends? Does she enjoy being part of that group? Does she fit in? Or does she try to keep you away from your friends? Does she want to keep you alone, with her, all the time?

"I can promise you one thing, young people," Jones said to all three of them. "If your boyfriend or girlfriend is constantly trying to keep you alone and away from your friends and family, something is wrong. This is a huge leaf you should pay attention to."

"A huge what?" Amelia asked. "A leaf?"

Jones stopped to explain. "Yes, a leaf. A leaf is an indicator. One can walk through the forest and never look up. But you can pick up a single leaf and know all sorts of information about the tree you are under. By examining a single leaf, you can tell the season of the year, whether the tree is large or small, whether it is poisonous or has fruit that you can eat ... yessir, you can tell a lot about a tree from a single leaf.

"You can tell a lot about a person from the leaves they drop as well. You don't have to be around someone a long time to know what their life is about. You can just examine the occasional leaf they drop. Believe me, that'll tell it all."

"Wow," Amelia said. "If this is all true—and I don't doubt that it is—then I seriously need to break up with my boyfriend."

"Better now than later, right, Jones?" Ritchie said.

Jones remained silent.

"Your boyfriend at the university?" Caroline asked.

Amelia nodded unhappily.

"Do your friends like him?"

"That wasn't the point," Ritchie said. "Remember?"

"I know," Caroline answered. "I was just . . . you know . . ."

"Actually," Amelia offered, "I don't *really* know *what* my friends think about him. I mean, *really* . . ."

"Our friends aren't always forthcoming about these matters," Jones said. "Often, they don't want to hurt our feelings, or maybe we filter any negative comments out because of our blind attraction to our boyfriend or girlfriend. A true friend will be honest with you, however, if you request it. Just be ready to listen. Sometimes we ignore the leaves piling up at our feet, while a true friend has managed to snag a few."

"This all seems so hard," Caroline said sadly.

"No, young lady," Jones responded, "it's really not. It's just different. Think this way for a bit and it will be the most natural thing in the world. Do you remember our definition of wisdom? *The ability to see into the future the consequences of your choices in the present.* Your family, your true friends, they have been placed in your life for a reason. They can help you gain perspective on whatever situation you're in. They are a resource. Pay attention."

Jones reached down, took Caroline's hand, and brought her to her feet. Amelia stood, and Ritchie thrust his right hand toward Jones. Their time was up.

"One more question," Ritchie said as he shook the old man's hand. Jones's eyebrows lifted in anticipation. "You know Emilio, right? The kid who works with the greens crew?"

"Yeah," Jones answered.

"Why does he call you Garcia?"

Jones grinned. "Why wouldn't he? Don't I look Hispanic to you?"

"Honestly," Ritchie said, "I always thought you were black."

"Does it make a difference?" Jones asked, looking from Ritchie to Caroline to Amelia.

"Well . . . no."

"No."

"Of course not."

Jones smiled broadly. "There you go, then," he said, as he stepped off the porch and sauntered across the parking lot.

Chapter 6

THE PINK AND PURPLE AZALEA BLOSSOMS WERE SO FULL
that they overpowered even the dogwoods and redbud, blocking
out any hint of the green leaves that lurked beneath them.
Seventy-six springs now, Willow Callaway had watched them
bloom. She moved slowly from her front porch, through the
yard to the road, and waited for the traffic to pass. Willow lived
on Canal Road, about a mile west of the big curve. Canal Road is
formally known as Highway 180, but only the tourists call it
that.

As she waited, the old woman thought back to when the
road was a simple dirt track. Now she had to stand and endure
the fumes and pace of people she hadn't asked to move here,
folks she didn't understand, who were loud and unappreciative
of the way things once were. Willow remembered when she and

her children would ease out of the house about this time of eve-ning and play by the banks of the canal. They would wave to the men on the barges and make up guessing games about the far-away places to which they were bound. Now the tugs and barges were air-conditioned, and nobody came outside to wave. Still, though, she sat and watched.

Willow stepped quickly across the road and moved toward the only bench within sight. It wasn't in a park. There was no light above it. No garbage can beside it. No fish-cleaning station or water hose or sign nearby about what was or wasn't permit-ted. Just a simple bench set beside another just like it. They sat side by side on a tiny dock no larger than fifteen feet square. Her husband had built the dock and benches decades ago.

By the time the small structure had been proudly placed on the canal bank, the children had already gone, leaving the house empty except for Willow and Bobby Gray, the man she married when she was sixteen. Many evenings were spent on one bench or the other—sitting there with a big glass of sweet iced tea between them, watching the slow-moving tide, talking about nothing—just being still and feeling God and loving each other, until he died.

Willow's oldest, Tommy, lived in Dallas now. He had chil-dren and even grandchildren of his own. Ray and Martha, the twins, were in Sarasota with the families they'd raised. Bradford, Willow's baby, was gone. Hard to believe she'd outlived one of her own children, but she had. Brad was only forty-seven when he died; she still thought of him as her baby. Yes, he was a grown man to some, but to her he had always been the sweet child who ran barefoot, tripping through the honeysuckle vines, who laughed at silly jokes but cried at Christmas that one year, so sad for baby Jesus because he had to be born in a barn.

She was proud of what she had accomplished, of the life she had led, but her life was over, and it was time to go. That was a fact she had decided months ago—knew it for certain—yet here she was, hanging around like somebody's forgotten holiday wreath, still on the front door in March. But, not inclined to take the matter into her own hands, Willow waited.

"Oh! Excuse me!" she said. Willow had not seen the old man sitting on her dock as she approached. And it was *her* dock. Even the mayor of Orange Beach had said so in a newspaper article one time. Everyone in town knew her husband had built it, and the dock was right across from her house. No car ever stopped there. No one else ever used it. The city mowed around it for her. It was the Willow Callaway Dock.

She had been so enthralled with the azaleas, never suspecting another person might be there, that the old man had taken her quite by surprise. He stood and smiled. "It's a lovely evening," he said, "and the location—extraordinary—a view to match!" Then, bowing slightly, he added, "Please, Mrs. Callaway ... do sit down. I can leave if you wish to be alone, but I would love to join you for a time, if I may."

"Sir," Willow said, "I find myself at a disadvantage ... for you obviously know who I am, yet I don't believe I have had the pleasure of being introduced."

He bowed again, this time offering his hand. "I do apologize, beautiful lady. You are well known in these parts, while I am but a raconteur, a traveling gentleman without means, a common drifter. My name is Jones, madam. Not *Mr.* Jones, if you will humor me—just plain Jones."

Willow smiled and held out her hand, allowing the very polite old man to help her to the bench on the right. "And may I join you?" he asked.

"Yes," Willow answered graciously, "please do."

They settled onto the small bench, Willow crossing her legs at the ankles and folding her hands in her lap, while Jones placed his suitcase on the planks at their feet. "I was admiring the woodwork," Jones said patting the seat between them. "An outstanding example of care not often seen today. I am told your late husband is to be credited for this fine bench?"

Willow beamed with pride. "Yes," she said, "my Bobby Gray built this in 1969. All pegs and notches. Not a nail in it, you'll notice."

"Yes, I did notice," Jones replied, touching the joints with his fingers. "Beautiful. Just beautiful."

"Am I to assume you are not a local?" Willow asked.

"You are correct," Jones answered. "I am not, but through the years, I have been here enough to know the area, love the people, and appreciate this bench."

Willow laughed warmly. "Well, you are certainly welcome here . . . Jones, I believe you said?"

"Yes, ma'am. And thank you."

Willow leaned out and pointed to her right, past Jones, into the water. "Do you see that big rock?" she asked.

"I do."

"It's low tide now. You can see it. Most times it's underwater. About five feet out from that rock, there's a big hole. The water's not so deep there, but the redfish group up in it when the tide's running hard. My boys took many a meal out of that old hole. Nobody knows about it now—boats running all around—but I still see those big old red drum sticking their tails up, rooting around the bottom for crabs and shrimp. Boats don't ever stop though . . ."

"You mentioned children," Jones said. "I assume they are grown and away. Do they visit often?"

"As much as they can. I don't expect them to, really." She turned as if amazed. "Did you know every one of my children has grandchildren? I never thought I'd be so old," Willow said. "Don't know when it happened. Probably when Brad died. Brad was my baby," she explained. "Not really a baby . . . almost fifty . . . but still . . ."

Both were silent for a bit before Willow spoke again. "It didn't hit me so hard when Bobby Gray passed, but a mama ought not to outlive her children . . . seems a cruel thing." Willow's lip quivered, and her voice broke. "I have outlived my usefulness. How in the world did I get so old?" She sniffed hard, then stuck her chin in the air. "Listen to me," she said. "Going on like a crazy person. I apologize. You must think I am terribly rude."

"No, no," Jones said gently. "Not at all. I do not think you rude in the least. *Wrong* maybe, but certainly not rude."

Willow turned sharply, not sure she had heard correctly. "I beg your pardon?"

Jones smiled and chose his words carefully. "My dear lady, I would banish from the realm of possibility that you might ever be rude; however"—Jones held a finger in the air—"when you make a statement so patently ridiculous as 'I have outlived my usefulness'"—he shrugged—"I fear I must openly disagree."

Willow turned and looked back at the water. "You are kind to say so," she said.

"But you don't believe me?" Jones asked, knowing the answer.

Willow was too polite to stand up and walk away or even to suggest he mind his own business, but for goodness' sake! She was aghast that a man she did not even know possessed the gall to dispute her conclusions about her own life. Then, to press the matter! "Sir," she said, a bit flustered, "I am an old woman wishing merely to live out my days without being in the way of those who still have much to do."

Jones raised his arms and looked upward. "Oh, Lord," he said, "don't let this old person die on this bench beside me." Holding the pose, he peered at Willow from the corners of his eyes.

"Don't tease," she said, and he chuckled softly.

"Well then," Jones said, "*you* be serious. You aren't *that* old. How old do you think *I* am?" Jones paused as she looked at him.

"Come on, now . . . think about it. Look me over. How old do you think I am?"

"I have no idea," Willow said.

"Well then," Jones said good-humoredly, "you're a winner for sure, 'cause I haven't got any idea either!" They both laughed; then Jones added, "I quit counting on the fiftieth anniversary of my thirty-ninth birthday!"

Willow shook her head. "Do you really not know?"

"Oh, I'm sure I could call it within a couple of decades," Jones said, "but what's the point? Should we let a number dictate how we feel? Besides, young lady—and I *do* consider you a young lady—who gave you permission to decide that you had nothing more to do, nothing more to offer?"

"Well," Willow said, "that is just an honest look at things. After Bobby passed away, and with the children living lives of their own . . ." Willow trailed off, but then, as if trying to convince herself, said with an air of finality, "There is only so much bridge one can play, and after all, isn't it the duty of the old to make way for the young? I simply feel that my time has passed."

"Wooowee!" Jones said in a high-pitched voice as he slapped his knees with both hands. "And aren't we glad everybody doesn't feel that way! The world would surely have missed out on some grand achievements."

"Mr. Jones," Willow said, trying not to smile, "you are teasing again."

"Well, I am and I ain't," he countered, "and it's just Jones. But let me give you a different perspective about feeling that your time has passed. Isn't it a good thing that Harlan Sanders didn't retire when he turned sixty-five?"

The name didn't register with Willow. "Harlan Sanders?"

"You probably remember him as *Colonel* Sanders. But it wasn't until he was sixty-five that he took a family recipe and began franchising restaurants to serve his fried chicken. And all he had at the time was his Social Security checks to get started— one hundred and five dollars a month."

"I didn't know that," Willow said. "Sixty-five, was he? Pretty good for a young person."

Jones chuckled. "I thought you might see it that way . . . Well, what about Benjamin Franklin? He didn't invent bifocals until he was seventy-eight. Winston Churchill was also seventy-eight and finished with more than a couple of careers when he wrote a book that won the Nobel Prize for Literature. Want me to continue?" Then, without so much as another breath, he said, "Nelson Mandela was inaugurated president of South Africa for the first time—after years in that country's prisons—at the age of seventy-five. Igor Stravinsky was still doing concerts when he was eighty-seven. Grandma Moses, the artist, did not sell her *first* painting until she was ninety. Michelangelo didn't *begin* his work on St. Peter's Basilica—one of the world's greatest treasures—until he was seventy-two."

"Stop!" Willow ordered, throwing up a hand and trying her best to stifle a smile. "How long could you go on with a list like this?"

"How much time do you have?"

"I suppose that's what we have been talking about," Willow replied, "how much time I have." Frowning suddenly, she said, "Only . . ."

"Only what?" Jones prompted.

"Only . . . I seem to have come to a lonely, fearful place. I have lived quite a few years myself, you know. And . . . trying not to make more of it than it is . . . this is the worst time in my life."

"Would you like logical proof that things will get better?" Jones asked.

"Oh, come on," Willow scoffed. "Does proof like that really exist?"

"Of course it does," Jones answered earnestly. "Many of life's treasures remain hidden from us simply because we never search for them. Often we do not ask the proper questions that might lead us to the answer to all our challenges. We are so caught up in fear and regret, that hope seems a foolish endeavor. *Proof of hope*, however, is not only possible; it is an overlooked law of the universe."

"Okay," Willow relented. "You have my attention."

"First," Jones began, looking down at his weather-beaten hands, "even during trying times, it is important to understand that such times are a normal part of life's ebb and flow—nothing to be too alarmed about. After all, every one of us is always *in* a crisis, *coming out of* a crisis, or *headed for* a crisis. Crisis? That's just part of being on this planet." Then, suddenly turning to face her, Jones said, "Take a deep breath."

"Excuse me?" she said.

"Come on, now . . . a big one. A big, *deeeeeep* breath."

As Willow's shoulders rose and then fell, she looked at Jones questioningly. "What does that tell you?" he said when she had exhaled.

"Well . . . uhhh . . . that the air is clean."

"No, no," Jones said enthusiastically. "More basic. Give me a literal view. What is the fundamental thing we know about people who can breathe?"

"That they are alive?"

"Correct!" Jones exulted. "That they are alive! Therefore, what might we ascertain from the fact that *you* can breathe?"

"That I am alive?" Willow said, a bit more certain this time of her answer.

"That is correct," Jones said. "And with that realization, we have the beginning of a chain of simple, unvarnished truths about your existence on this earth. Your very breath provides authentic and infallible absolutes that cannot be disputed. Here, my friend, even during what you may consider the worst time in your life, is proof of hope. Incidentally, this proof is genuine regardless of a person's age, physical condition, financial situation, color, gender, emotional state, or belief. Now, listen closely . . .

"If you are breathing, you are still alive. If you are alive, then you are still here, physically, on this planet. If you are still here, then you have not completed what you were put on earth to do. If you have not completed what you were put on earth to do . . . that means your very *purpose* has not yet been fulfilled. If your purpose has not yet been fulfilled, then the *most important part of your life* has not yet been lived. And if the most important part of your life has not yet been lived . . ." Jones paused, waiting for Willow to follow his thought to conclusion.

"That is my proof of hope," Willow said softly.

"Yes, it is," Jones agreed. "If the most important part of your life is ahead of you, then, even during the worst times, one can be assured that there is more laughter ahead, more success to look forward to, more children to teach and help, more friends to touch and influence. There is proof of hope . . . for more."

They were silent for a time before Willow spoke again. "Where do I begin? How do I start?" she said quietly. "Don't misunderstand me, Jones. I am old, but not hardheaded. I am convinced"—she smiled shyly—"*and* excited. I'd like to accomplish *some*thing, even though I know it won't be a big thing. It would be nice to know I am at least making a tiny difference."

Jones pursed his lips and looked at Willow warily. "How would you react," he said, "if I disagreed with you twice in one day?"

Taken by surprise, the old woman opened her eyes wide. "What did I say this time?" she asked in disbelief.

Jones took a breath and blew it out noisily. Shaking his head, he said, "That part about a 'tiny' difference?"

"Yes? What was wrong with that? Surely, I can make a *tiny* difference!"

Shaking his head, Jones said, "Sorry, but I've never known a single person who ever made a tiny difference. I am not even convinced it is possible. So, *you* will have to settle for making a huge difference."

Intrigued, Willow cocked her head. "Go on . . ."

"While it is true that most people never see or understand the difference they make, or sometimes only *imagine* their actions having a tiny effect, every single action a person takes has far-reaching consequences.

"A moment ago, you and I were talking about particular people who had accomplished great things during the later years of their lives. Do you know the name Norman Borlaug?" Willow shook her head. "Norman Borlaug was ninety-one when he was informed that he had been personally responsible for saving the lives of two billion people."

"Two billion people?" Willow exclaimed. "How is that possible?"

"Norman Borlaug was the man who hybridized corn and wheat for arid climates," Jones answered. "The Nobel committee, the Fulbright Scholars, and many other experts calculated that all across the world—in Central and South America, Western Africa, across Europe and Asia, throughout the plains of Siberia, and America's own desert Southwest—Borlaug's work has saved from famine over two billion people . . . and the number is increasing every day."

"Incredible," Willow said.

"Yes," Jones agreed. "Isn't it? But the most incredible part of the story is that Borlaug, for all the credit he has received . . ." Jones glanced around as if to prevent someone from hearing what he was about to say. "For all the credit he's received, Borlaug was *not* the person who saved the two billion people."

"What?"

"That's right," Jones confirmed. "I believe it was a man named Henry Wallace. He was vice president of the United States under Roosevelt."

"I thought Truman was vice president under Roosevelt," Willow said suspiciously.

"He was," Jones agreed, "but remember, Roosevelt served four terms. His first two terms, John Nance served as vice president; his fourth term, Truman; but it was during Roosevelt's third term that his vice president was a former secretary of agriculture named Henry Wallace. While Wallace was vice president of the United States, he used the power of his office to create a station in Mexico whose sole purpose was to somehow hybridize corn and wheat for arid climates . . . and he hired a young man named Norman Borlaug to run it. So, while Norman Borlaug won the Nobel Prize . . . it was really Henry Wallace whose initial act was responsible for saving the two billion lives."

"I never knew," Willow said. "Why, I don't even remember the man."

"That's okay," Jones replied. "Now that I think about it, maybe it wasn't Henry Wallace who should've gotten credit anyway . . ."

Willow appeared startled. "Now, why would you say *that*?" she asked.

Jones dropped his eyes to the ground and rubbed his chin, as if deep in thought. "Maybe it was George Washington Carver who saved the two billion lives." Then, his head popping up again, he said, "You remember him, don't you?"

"Yes," Willow answered quickly. "Peanuts. But what does he—"

"What people don't know about George Washington Carver is that while he was nineteen and a student at Iowa State University, he had a dairy sciences professor who allowed his own six-year-old boy to go on botanical expeditions every weekend with this brilliant student. George Washington Carver took that little tot and directed his life. And it was Carver who gave six-year-old *Henry Wallace* a vision about his future and what he could do with plants to help humanity."

Jones shook his head in wonder. "It is amazing, isn't it?" he said. "That Carver could spend all that time with the peanut? Hours and months and years of work. I mean, the man developed two hundred and sixty-six products from the peanut—that we still use today. And then there's the sweet potato. *Eighty-eight* uses he developed from it." Jones leaned forward, hands on his knees. "He also wrote an agricultural tract and promoted the idea of what he called a 'victory garden.'"

Willow smiled. "I remember victory gardens. We had one."

"Yes. So did most people," Jones said. "Victory gardens—even in the middle of major cities—fed a significant portion of our population during World War II.

"But with all the time and effort and years that Carver spent on things like peanuts and sweet potatoes and victory gardens, isn't it amazing that a few afternoons with a six-year-old boy named Henry Wallace turned out to make *that* much difference!"

"Truly," Willow said with awe in her voice. "So it *was* George Washington Carver whose action saved all those people."

"Ahhh . . . ," Jones shook his head. "Not really."

"*What?*"

"It had to have been the farmer from Diamond, Missouri." Jones grinned as Willow threw up her hands.

"There was a farmer in Diamond, Missouri, named Moses," Jones continued, "who had a wife named Susan. They lived in a slave state but didn't believe in slavery. Well, that was a problem for those crazy people who rode through farms at night, terrorizing what they called 'sympathizers.' And one cold winter night, Quantrill's Raiders attacked Moses and Susan's farm. They burned the barn, shot several people, and dragged off a woman named Mary Washington . . . who refused to let go of her infant son, George.

"Now, Mary Washington was Susan's best friend, so Moses sent word out immediately, trying to arrange a meeting with those cutthroats, trying to do something to get Mary and her baby back. Within a few days, he had the meeting set; and so, on a January night, Moses took a black horse and went several hours north to a crossroads in Kansas.

"There, he met four of Quantrill's men, who arrived on horseback, carrying torches, wearing flour sacks with eyeholes cut out over their heads. And Moses traded his only horse for what they threw him in a burlap bag.

"As they thundered off, Moses fell to his knees. There, in the freezing dark, with his breath's vapor blowing hard and white from his mouth, Moses brought out of that burlap bag a cold, naked, almost dead baby boy. And he opened up his jacket and he opened up his shirts and placed that baby next to his skin. Moses fastened that child in under his clothes and walked that baby out! Talking to that child every step of the way—telling the baby he would take care of him and raise him as his own . . . promising to educate him to honor Mary, his mother, who they knew was already dead."

Jones looked intently at Willow who stared back in wonder. "That was the night," he said softly, "that the farmer told that baby he would give him his name. And *that* is how Moses and Susan Carver came to raise that little baby, George Washington.

"So there. It was obviously the farmer from Diamond, Missouri, who saved those two billion people."

They sat quietly for a moment until Jones raised his finger as if an idea had just come to him. Teasing, he said, "Unless maybe . . ." But then, seeing the tears in Willow's eyes, he said, "So you see, madam, we could continue this line of reasoning all evening. For the truth is, who knows who it really was whose single action saved the two billion people? How far back could we go?" Jones reached over and took Willow's hand. "And how far into the future could we go, dear lady, to show how many lives *you* will touch? There are generations yet unborn, whose very lives will be shifted and shaped by the moves you make and the actions you take . . . tonight. And tomorrow. And tomorrow night. And the next day. And the next.

"No matter your age, physical condition, financial situation, color, gender, emotional state, or belief . . . everything you do, every move you make, matters to all of us—and forever."

"Thank you," Willow said faintly. "Thank you."

"And thank *you*, young lady," Jones said as he stood. "Thank you for the opportunity to spend a few moments with you and rest in such a beautiful spot." He began walking slowly westward, toward the canal. "Let's not rest too long, though," Willow heard him say as the evening darkness took him from her sight. "Time is precious, and you have much to do."

Chapter 7

MY BOYS CLIMBED INTO MY LAP. THE SIX-YEAR-OLD SPOKE first. "Mr. Jones sure is nice."

"He is, isn't he?" I responded. Jones had left only minutes earlier, having spent the evening with Polly, the boys, and me and, as always, declining an invitation to stay the night.

"I *love* Mr. Jones," said our four-year-old.

"I do too, buddy," I replied. "Hey, did you guys call him Jones? Or *Mr.* Jones?"

"*Mr.* Jones," they both answered solemnly. Then our oldest added, "He said we could call him just plain Jones, but I told him that we might get in trouble if we didn't say 'mister' for somebody that old!"

I silently gave thanks that Jones was not a woman. "What did he say to that?" I asked.

"He just laughed," my toddler answered. "Then he kind of scruffled our hair and bumped our heads together. Real soft, though. It didn't hurt."

I was grateful that my family had at last been able to meet the old man. He had been in town for almost six weeks, and I was beginning to despair that I might not have any more time alone with him. Three or four cups of coffee—always unexpectedly and on the spur of the moment—were the only encounters it seemed we would have. Then, of course, there was the tree house . . .

I was the first one of my family to be up and around that morning. As I left the kitchen door to make the brief outdoor walk to my office, I stopped and literally rubbed my eyes in disbelief. There, perched in the six palm trees beside our home, was a tree house that had not been there the afternoon before.

Suffice it to say, I was stunned. Trust me—this was no ordinary tree house. The construction looked like something straight out of *Swiss Family Robinson* and had not the slightest relation to the plywood platforms I had nailed precariously to the branches of the nearest oak when I was a boy. In fact, there didn't seem to be a nail in the entire structure. Bamboo, rope, and thatch appeared to be woven seamlessly into what can only be described as a child's dream home.

As I stood there with my mouth open, Jones stuck his head through the tree house doorway. Grinning broadly, he said, "Join me," and extended a hand to guide me up the ladder. "Do you think they'll like it?"

"Who?" I asked dumbly.

"Your boys!" Jones laughed. "Will they like it?"

Reaching the tiny porch, I said, "My gosh . . . they'll love it. How did you do this? *When* did you do this?"

"Oh, I had plenty of time," he chuckled. "And Claire and Scott helped me. AmaZuluInc.com had all the materials. You've heard of the Internet?"

I peered at him suspiciously and he laughed so hard that I thought he might fall off the tree house. "Remember Andy," he finally said. "you can do whatever you want to do. You can accomplish whatever you want to accomplish. You are never lacking funds. Neither is the calendar your enemy. When you need most to accomplish something great in your life, you are only lacking an idea. Time and money, my friend, are also a matter of perspective."

Anyway, I never did find out how he did it. Claire and Scott, I learned later, worked with AmaZuluInc.com, a company that imports unusual materials for companies like Disney or Sea World, but they both swore they were nowhere around that night and had not even heard of a client named Jones. The boys, as you might imagine, did love the tree house. They still play in it every day.

About that time, I was also increasingly aware of just how strange it seemed to hear stories about "Jones sightings" from people in the area who didn't even know that we were acquainted. He was beginning to create a bit of a stir.

Almost everywhere he appeared, because of his reputation

for honesty and wisdom dispensed with a healthy dose of humor, a crowd would gather to ask questions and listen closely to his answers. Everyone seemed to emerge from those encounters with a new perspective on their situation, which allowed them to regroup, take a breath, and begin their lives again from a different point of view. We also heard about individuals who managed to talk with him one-on-one. Most of these conversations, it seemed, were almost eerie in the coincidence of place and time that brought Jones into each person's life. The stories reminded me of my first encounter with him, that night under the pier so long ago.

Earlier in the day, I had passed a business on the beach that displayed a huge sign. In the largest letters available, the owner had placed a quote from Jones for everyone to see. The old man had spoken the words during a conversation with several people about the hurricane devastation suffered by the Gulf Coast over the past several years. A friend had already told me what he said, and folks around here were repeating it to one another, but to see Jones's words on the huge sign seemed amazing. It read:

Rebuild with a grateful heart. You may have lost a house, but you did not lose your home. Remember, you are still breathing . . .

Jones

I laughed when I heard he had been to a local church (I won't say which one), and when the pastor asked if there were any prayer requests, Jones stood up and said, "I'd like us to pray for some smiling faces in this church." Then, in typical fashion, he added, "I think more people would want to go to heaven, if they weren't afraid it'd be like church when they got there!"

It was amazing, really. Jones merely told the truth, and without exception, people accepted what he said with open minds and good humor. Even the hardest hearts seemed to melt in his presence.

HENRY WARREN LEFT ATLANTA JUST AFTER MIDNIGHT, headed for the coast. He drove through Montgomery with no radio or CD playing. In silence, just before five o'clock, he took the first Bay Minette exit off I-65 and turned south on Highway 59, toward the beach. Henry was thirty-two years old and married to a wife he rarely saw, who was pregnant with their first child. They lived in Buckhead, a suburb of Atlanta, in a townhome they struggled to afford—this in addition to a two-bedroom condo on the beach.

Financially, Henry was nowhere near where he wanted to be, and even though he was a "big-picture guy" and a tireless worker, sometimes he wondered if he was beating his head against the wall and didn't know it. On most occasions, however, he was quickly able to put those kinds of thoughts out of his mind and forge ahead.

Henry considered himself the ultimate entrepreneur. In addition to an advertising firm in Atlanta, where he employed five people, Henry owned a landscaping business at the beach and operated two crews of anywhere from three to seven, depending on the job. He drove a leased Chevy Tahoe, two years old, with seventy thousand miles already on it—most of those back and forth between Atlanta and the coast.

Henry drove the hour south on Highway 59 with his window open, trying to stay awake, until he came to the dead end at the gulf. Taking a right onto West Beach Boulevard, he saw the sun coming over the horizon in his rearview mirror. Henry glanced at the clock in his dashboard: 6:10. There was not enough time to go by his own place, but he had a few minutes to rest before meeting both crews at the new condominium job he had recently bid for and won. And it was a job that would take both crews, he knew.

Henry had promised the developer that all palms, shrubs, flowering plants, sod, and irrigation would be in place and complete within six days. It was a massive undertaking and one he knew there was no chance of finishing on time. But at that point, he reasoned, the job was already his, and the developer would have no choice but to let him finish.

As Henry slid the Tahoe into a parking place and cut off the engine, he mentally debated whether to sleep for a few minutes or work on the bid for another project due later that day. Before reaching a conclusion, Henry fell into a fitful sleep.

Henry's business life was a juggling act. He never did anything overtly illegal—as long as one didn't count the undocumented workers—but a graduate course in ethics could have written a curriculum based on the corners Henry cut on a daily basis. There would always be plenty of work, though, he reasoned, for the person who kept his eye on the big picture.

The "big picture" for Henry involved signing contracts with as many clients as he could possibly sign. And to get them, he promised timetables that could never be met, materials he would never actually use, and quality he would never deliver. His modus operandi was simply to get the job started to establish his "claim," then hit each work site enough during the week for the client to see *some* progress. He dealt with any complaints and frustrations by assigning blame elsewhere and making more promises he knew were impossible to keep.

Eventually, the job would be finished, and Henry would be paid in full; but by that time, clients were so tired of the process that they were glad to see Henry go—not that he cared. (After all, there was plenty of work—and plenty of customers—for the person who kept his eye on the big picture.) When Henry paid his crews, he usually shorted them, adding the curt explanation that they had not completed the job to his satisfaction. After all, he knew, most of them were illegals—to whom would *they* complain?

Henry awoke with a start in the middle of another bad dream. Bad dreams were all he had anymore—the product, Henry assumed, of a lack of sleep. Checking his watch as he hurried out the door of the big Chevy, the young businessman saw that it was almost eight o'clock. The crews should have started an hour ago.

Henry strode purposefully across the parking lot to where an eighteen-wheeler sat loaded with palm trees. Several workers were standing around with shovels in their hands while one tinkered with a tractor that was not yet running. Henry cursed loudly, and the crew looked his way. "What are you people doing?" he screamed. "These trees should've already been unloaded! You aren't being paid to stand around. Two of you stay here. The rest of you . . . dig the marked holes!" He cursed again as the workers scattered.

By midmorning, the trees were unloaded, and eleven workers—men and women—were spread across the property, feverishly and fearfully doing their jobs. Henry divided his time between haranguing the crews and dealing with his other, neglected clients on the cell phone. The only calls he didn't answer were the ones from his wife. He was simply too busy and knew she would understand.

Walking to the far corner of the property, Henry began to track the irrigation lines from the well. "Hey!" he called to the workers ahead of him. "Don't take all day trenching the lines so deep. Just get 'em covered with sand. Five inches is as good as fifteen."

"Sir?" came a voice from behind Henry.

"What?" Henry answered without turning around.

"Sir, if we don't bury the lines deeply, the wind will have them all uncovered in less than a month."

"We won't be here in a month."

"No sir, we won't," the voice responded. "Only thing left

here for everyone to see will be a bunch of uncovered irrigation lines . . . and your reputation."

In a fury, Henry wheeled on whoever had dared to speak to him that way. "Who in the hell do you think—" He froze, seeing an old man in front of him, with the bluest eyes he had ever encountered. The crystalline gaze seemed to hold Henry in place, and for a moment, the young man felt as though he might pass out. Regaining a degree of composure, Henry managed to croak, "Do you work for me?"

"I always have," the old man replied with a smile.

It seemed an odd answer from someone whom Henry was certain he had never seen. Yet, in another way, the old man was vaguely familiar. All the anger drained from Henry in an instant. In its place was an overwhelming sense of confusion. "Tell me your name again?"

"Jones. And I know you prefer to be called Mr. Warren, but just for today, may I address you as a friend?"

Henry nodded dumbly. Was he getting sick? he wondered. He felt light-headed—aware of a strange presence in this old man, manifested from his eyes, that took Henry's focus from everything but his face and the sound of his voice.

"Let's move to the shade, okay?" Jones suggested, motioning to a large oak tree nearby. "I want to ask you a couple of questions."

"But the work . . ." Henry gestured feebly toward the crews and their frantic activity.

"The work will get done," Jones said, peering across the

property. "But this is an important day for you . . . and we need to talk." The old man moved the battered suitcase he held to his opposite hand and reached up to drape his arm across Henry's shoulders, guiding him gently to the relative privacy of the oak. Henry, for his part, did not want to go, did not know *why* he was going, but walked in step with the old man, without a word of disagreement.

"Sit here," Jones said as Henry obligingly eased himself to the ground. "Can I get you some water?" Henry shook his head.

It was as if he were emerging from a fog. Henry's brain was firing in several different directions at once. *I am so tired. I followed this old man over here to . . . What am I supposed to do? I am here to talk? About what?*

"Young man?"

Henry looked at Jones, who had lain the suitcase on its side and settled cross-legged on top of it, directly in front of him.

"Young man . . . do you hear me?"

"Yes, sir," he answered, wondering as he spoke why the old man was talking so loudly. His voice seemed to drown out the sounds of the traffic on the road and the machinery on the property behind him. "Yes, sir," he said again. "I can hear you."

Suddenly, Henry felt a wave of panic wash over him. *What is happening? Who is this man? Am I sick? Why can't I get up?* Just as quickly, Jones placed his hand on Henry's arm, and the younger man felt tension leave his body in a rush. "Who are you?" Henry asked somewhat fearfully. "What do you want from me?"

Jones released Henry's arm and patted it a couple of times before pulling away. "I am here to deliver some bad news," he answered. Then, leaning forward, Jones said, "Soon, you will be dead."

Henry was already in such a state that his physical reaction was minimal, though everything inside him both screamed and scrambled to leave this man and this place. Instead, he whispered, "I don't understand."

"Life is a breath, a passing breeze; a blade of grass, green and vibrant for a time, only to wither, die, and disappear. Soon you will be dead. And after the funeral, Henry Warren's friends and family will gather to eat fried chicken and banana pudding. They will say the same things about him that they say about any other person for whom they didn't really care. Why? Because life is like a game of Monopoly. You may own hotels on Boardwalk or you may be renting on Baltic Avenue. But in the end, it all goes back in the box. The next generation will be getting out all your stuff and playing with it or fighting over it.

"Son, I've heard you many times refer to the 'big picture,' but you need to hear from me—now—that the big picture you have in *your* head is leading you to a desperate life of hurt and darkness."

As Henry listened, the fog in his brain lifted. Though he seemed unable to tear his eyes from the old man's own, he was hearing and comprehending every word Jones spoke. "You said that soon I would be dead . . ." Henry started carefully.

"Merely an attention getter," Jones replied, "but an interesting perspective on life, wouldn't you agree, and no less an absolute fact in your case than in the lives of everyone around you." Jones waved his hand, taking in all the people in his view. "They will all be dead soon too. In fact," he added with a twinkle in his eye, "in dog years, most of them are *already* dead!"

Henry shook his head as if to clear it. "What are we talking about here? I still don't understand."

"I know you don't," Jones said with a gentle smile. "Let's see if we can't clear some things up." He paused for a moment, then asked, "Have you ever heard the saying 'Don't sweat the small stuff'?"

"Yes," Henry responded.

"Well," Jones said, "I'm here to tell you that you'd better. See, the 'small stuff' is what makes up the larger picture of our lives. Many people are like you, young man. But their perspective is distorted. They ignore 'small stuff,' claiming to have an eye on the bigger picture, never understanding that the bigger picture is composed of nothing more than—are you ready?—'small stuff.'

"Have you ever been bitten by an elephant?" the old man asked. Henry shook his head. "How about a mosquito?" Jones offered.

"Of course," Henry answered.

"You see what I mean?" Jones said, reaching out to cuff Henry on the shoulder. "It's the small stuff that'll get you!"

Henry smiled in spite of himself.

"A few years ago," Jones said, leaning back onto his elbows, "a squirrel climbed onto the Metro-North Railroad power lines near New York City. He set off an electrical surge, which weakened an overhead bracket. The bracket allowed a wire to dangle toward the tracks. The wire tangled in a train that tore down all the lines. As a result, forty-seven thousand commuters were stranded in Manhattan for hours that evening. And I'll bet it wasn't even a big squirrel.

"Remember the Hubble Space Telescope?" Jones continued. "It was conceived in 1946 and cost $2.5 billion to produce. Yet when it was launched into orbit, NASA discovered that a particular lens had been ground $1/1000^{th}$ of an inch less than it should have been. That 'little thing,' until it was repaired by astronauts, rendered the most expensive telescope in history no better than a good one on the ground."

Jones watched Henry carefully to be certain he was listening. "My point, young man—at least for the beginning of our discussion—is that you'd be wise to sweat the small stuff. Little things *do* matter. Take Napoleon, for instance; a tiny part of the battle became immensely important to Napoleon when he defeated Wellington at Waterloo."

Henry frowned. "But Napoleon didn't win at Waterloo," he said. "It was his greatest defeat."

"Are you sure?" Jones asked.

"Yes. Absolutely."

Jones nodded in concession. "You are correct, young man. On the eighteenth of June 1815, Napoleon did indeed suffer his greatest defeat—an unmitigated disaster—at Waterloo. But that was only after he won!" Jones chortled at the skeptical look on Henry's face and said, "Here is the story that very few know . . .

"Napoleon had brilliantly outmaneuvered Wellington's 77,000 men—this in addition to the more than 100,000 Prussians nearby. Together, those armies easily outnumbered Napoleon's 76,000, but when he got in between them, Napoleon prevented the two from combining. He had already beaten the Prussians two days before, so he detached a part of his force to hold them at bay while pointing the rest of his army toward Wellington and the British.

"Napoleon began the battle at a bit after eleven in the morning with an artillery barrage and an initial assault against the British right flank. Pushing back and forth most of the day, at one point Napoleon watched from a hillside as his troops pushed past Wellington's lines, capturing almost all of the 160 British cannons."

Jones stopped his story and asked, "Have you ever seen one of those cannons up close?"

"Yes," Henry answered. "A muzzle-loading cannon, right?"

"Correct. The cannons were packed with black gunpowder, wadding, and a projectile of some sort. The touchhole of the cannon was then contacted with a flaming torch, which ignited the powder and fired the cannon. Do you follow me?"

"Yes," Henry responded, unsure of just what he was supposed to follow.

Jones continued. "It was customary in those days for several of the troops to carry small metal rods—nails—with them in the event that they overran the enemy's guns. The metal rods were then hammered into the cannon's touchhole, rendering it useless. When Napoleon's men overran Wellington's position—and his cannons—it became immediately apparent that there were no spikes among his troops. As Napoleon screamed from the hilltop for the cannons to be destroyed, he watched Wellington's men retake the guns and turn them on their attackers. Napoleon was defeated . . . and all for lack of a fistful of nails."

"I have never heard that story," Henry said. "What are you trying to tell me?"

"That your 'big picture' will never be a masterpiece if you ignore the tiny brushstrokes. You are trying so hard to be successful that true success is eluding you. What pictures come into your mind when I say 'success'? Quickly . . . tell me."

"Well," Henry started, "a house . . . a *big* house. Nice cars. Vacations. An expensive watch. Jewelry for my wife. A boat, maybe several—"

"And now," Jones butted in before Henry could go any further, "what comes to mind when I say 'successful life'?"

Henry didn't immediately answer. But finally, with a shaken look, he answered. "My wife, my unborn child—it's a boy, you know."

Jones nodded. "I know. Keep going," he said.

"Time to spend with my family. Good friends. People in whose lives I have made a difference—"

"A *positive* difference?" Jones interrupted and watched as

Henry's face whitened. "I have a feeling you've already made a difference in a few lives . . ."

"That's probably true," Henry acknowledged with shame.

"No probably about it, young man," Jones said. "You are like many people," Jones told him, "one step away from a cliff you could avoid if you'd just take your blindfold off. Financially, physically, emotionally . . . in almost every area of your life you are chasing success, yet bulling toward disaster. And so far, I'm one of only two people who care enough to tell you. The other one at this point is still your wife, but you won't listen to her. You won't even answer her calls."

Henry looked hard at the old man. "How do you know that?"

"Am I wrong?" Receiving no reply, Jones looked toward the workers. "Can you tell me their names?" he asked. Henry shook his head. Jones pointed out the three closest, who were on their hands and knees, laying irrigation in the blazing sun. "Walter, Ramón, and Juanita.

"Walter is a grandfather. He has a son named William, who is an engineer with a wife and two children of their own. They lived in Detroit, but William was laid off a year ago. Soon after, one of the kids got sick. Now that family is back with Walter and his wife." Jones turned, scanning the property, his hand shading his eyes. He gestured toward a younger man digging a hole for a palm. "There's William. He works on your crew too.

"Ramón and Juanita are not yet parents, though they'd like

to be. They are actually the same age as you, young man, and your wife. Juanita had a miscarriage four days ago . . . on Saturday. Do you remember what you told Ramón on Monday morning?"

"He didn't tell me that she—"

"You told him that if his wife wasn't on the job that afternoon, they'd both be fired."

Jones held Henry's gaze for a moment, then looked around again. "Martin is the boy working the hose," Jones said, nodding in the boy's direction. "He is sixteen. This is his first job. His father owns half the real estate in this town. He wanted his son to get his own job and make his own way this summer. He could have worked at any number of businesses his father owns, but here he is. Martin has told his father what it's like to work for you, but so far, his father has encouraged him not to quit. I think his father is using you as an example for his son. He knows Martin will also be responsible for quite a few employees in the future. As long as you don't hit the boy, I think his father will keep him here, but young man . . . ?" Henry's eyes flickered up, "I don't think you'll be getting any glowing references from anyone associated with Martin's family.

"The three young fellows over there"—Henry turned to follow Jones's pointing finger. "There with the palm . . . Hugo, Ricardo, and Mario. They are from a small town south of the Texas border. Their father is dead. Their mother is sick—sick with *what*, they don't have the money to find out. They have a sister who is fifteen and dreams of one day going to college.

They came across the border a month ago and hitched a ride here. Less chance of getting caught in this area, they think." Jones paused, then added, "I'm not saying what they did was right. I'm just telling you who they are.

"Shirley and Letha are mother and daughter. They are at the watercooler, watching you. They look scared to death, don't they? Like you might yell at them for stopping for a drink . . ." Jones waited to see if Henry would say anything, but the younger man merely hung his head. "Something is wrong with Letha," Jones went on after a moment. "She's almost thirty, but has the mind of a twelve-year-old. Her husband left years ago. Shirley could qualify for any number of government programs, but she's simply too proud. This is only one of three jobs she holds down.

"Fred is the skinny guy holding the ditch digger. He's fifty and working a couple of jobs himself. He lives in an apartment with his mother. A good man, by all accounts, but devoid of hope. He lost it years ago. Fred probably doesn't work as hard as he could or should. Is that why you shorted him fifty dollars last week?" Jones lowered his head in order to make eye contact with Henry, who was staring at the ground.

"I paid him what he deserved," Henry offered feebly.

"That's probably true," Jones agreed. Then the old man's face hardened. "What about you, young man?" he asked flatly. "Would you like to get what you deserve?" Jones let that question hang in the air for a moment, then sighed, shook his head, and said, "Me? I surely don't want what I deserve. I'm hoping for mercy, not justice.

"These lives, these spirits—Walter and William, Shirley, Letha, Ramón, Juanita, and the rest—are just as precious to the One who made them as your unborn son is to you."

For a time, the two sat quietly, alone at the crossroads that Henry Warren's life had just reached. The old man was waiting and watching, as he had with so many others, for evidence of a decision. In Jones's experience, the decision to turn one's life in a different direction rarely arrived with fireworks and marching bands. Often, the decision came with tears and regret. Then, almost impossibly, the power of forgiveness would fill an unseen void, allowing a new day's optimism and sense of purpose to take hold and point that life in a new direction.

"My life is a mess," Henry said softly.

"Yes, it is," Jones agreed, "but only up to this moment."

The younger man looked up. "What do you mean?"

"I mean that you can change. Now. You can change how you do business, how you treat your family, and how you treat the people whose working lives have been entrusted to you. You can change how you treat them. *Right now.*"

Jones peered carefully into the eyes of the younger man as he continued. "Most people think it takes a long time to change. It doesn't. Change is immediate! Instantaneous! It may take a long time to *decide* to change . . . but *change* happens in a heartbeat!"

"Then I will change," Henry said. "I mean . . . I *am* changed."

"You understand, of course," Jones said, "that it might take a while for your reputation to catch up to the change you have already made?" Henry nodded. "Most folks will be in that 'deciding to change' mode in their opinions about *you* for some time yet. But the change you have made will show evidence of a different man, and sooner or later, others will change their feelings about you as well.

"One quick question," Jones said with an obvious lightening of the mood, "and to complete the change in all areas of your life, you will need to understand the answer. Are you ready?"

"Okay . . ." Henry said warily.

"Five seagulls are sitting on a dock. One of them decides to fly away. How many seagulls are left?"

"Well . . . four."

"No," Jones responded. "There are still five. Deciding to fly away and *actually* flying away are two very different things.

"Listen carefully to me. Despite popular belief to the contrary, there is absolutely no power in intention. The seagull may intend to fly away, may decide to do so, may talk with the other seagulls about how wonderful it is to fly, but until the seagull flaps his wings and takes to the air, he is still on the dock. There's no difference between that gull and all the others. Likewise, there is no difference in the person who *intends* to do things differently and the one who never thinks about it in the first place. Have you ever considered how often we judge ourselves by our intentions while we judge others by their actions? Yet intention without action is an insult to those who expect the best from you. 'I *intended* to bring you flowers, but I didn't.' 'I *meant* to finish this work on time.' 'I was *going* to be there for your birthday . . .'"

Henry felt overwhelmed but determined. "I get it, I think. Now, what do I do first?"

"If you have changed," Jones said, "show evidence of it." He pointed to the cell phone on Henry's belt and smiled. "First, call your wife. The rest you'll figure out."

Henry unclipped the phone, looked at Jones, and asked, "Right now?"

"Right now," the old man said as he stood and stretched.

Henry dialed the familiar number and waited for his wife to answer. When she did, his words came in a rush. "Honey! I am sorry for so many things. I promise things will be better. *I* will be better. I know I sound crazy right now, but we'll talk when I get home. I met a guy, and I want you to say hello. Hang on just a minute . . ." Henry looked up. He turned around, but the old man was gone. Baffled, Henry did a complete 360, scanning the site for a glimpse of old Jones, but he was nowhere to be seen.

But in that brief moment of confusion, Henry had no way of knowing that Jones was not through with him yet.

Chapter 8

SEVERAL DAYS HAD PASSED SINCE HIS CONVERSATION WITH the strange old man, and Henry Warren was discouraged. What he had thought would be a relatively smooth process of converting people to the "new" Henry was anything but. He had tried to apologize to everyone he had openly offended, with little success. One man had taken the opportunity to tell Henry just what he thought of him . . . and his apology. Even Henry's wife was having a hard time adjusting.

As for Henry, determination had never been a problem for him. He remained convinced that *something* had happened to him that day with Jones under the oak tree. He was truly a different man, he believed. Unfortunately, no one seemed willing to give him the benefit of the doubt.

On this particular morning, Henry was on his hands and

knees, finishing the last of the irrigation so that the sod could be laid at the condominium's entrance. He was working beside Ramón and had insisted that Juanita rest in his truck during the heat of the day.

It is Thursday, Ramón thought. *He has been like this since Monday, when Garcia left. And Mr. Warren has ordered Juanita to rest?* Neither Ramón nor Juanita understood exactly what was happening, but they had never seen Henry actually work with them either. All they had known from this man had been curses and threats. Now this? And who was the old man Ricardo and Hugo had told him was named Garcia? What did he have to do with all this?

"You sure are burying those lines awfully deep," a familiar voice said.

Henry looked up, almost afraid to hope . . . but sure enough, there he was. "Jones!" he said excitedly as he scrambled to his feet. "Man! I'm glad to see you! And, by the way, we are burying them deeper than I told the developer we would."

"Good for you," the old man said, obviously pleased.

"Can you spare a minute?" Henry asked. "I didn't know how to reach you, and . . . well . . . I need to talk."

"Sure," Jones said. "I thought you might have a few questions by now."

Henry patted Ramón on the back with a smile and pointed him toward his wife and the watercooler. "Break," he said. "Good work, Ramón. Take fifteen minutes, okay?"

Jones almost laughed out loud at the combination of happiness and confusion coming together on Ramón's face as he tried to understand this "new" boss. To Henry, Jones motioned toward the shade of the oak and said, "Our tree?"

"Fine," Henry agreed and reached for the old man's suitcase. "Let me carry that for you."

"No, no," Jones said, laughing, as he swung it out of Henry's reach. "I'm old. Don't make me out to be feeble too!" And he turned and trudged purposefully toward their "meeting room" under the tree. Henry followed.

As they settled on the ground, Henry couldn't have been happier. He was thrilled that the old man had shown up again. It was almost a physical change he noticed in himself when Jones was around. But soon Henry grew somber as he remembered what he wanted to say. Jones didn't miss Henry's change of expression.

"How are you doing?" Jones asked.

"Good. Fine," Henry answered, then scrunched up his face. "Or not good. I don't really know."

"Tell me," Jones urged.

"I have apologized to several—actually, quite a few—people. My wife first, of course. Some suppliers and developers. All my crew here. Every one of them, Jones! But . . . they don't seem to be okay with me. There is still a distance—even with my wife. Heck, *especially* with my wife! You know, she's seven months pregnant . . . I'd like to get this settled before the baby is born."

Jones smiled sympathetically. "I know. And wouldn't it be great if everything and everybody responded to our personal timetable." Henry opened his mouth to speak again, but Jones cut him off. "Listen, young man, you spent years creating your reputation—the image of you that people hold in their minds and hearts. It might take more than a few days to turn it all around." Jones closed one eye and held up a finger. "It might even be a bit more challenging than you thought at first."

Henry swallowed and steeled himself for what Jones might say next.

Jones noticed. "Henry," he said, grinning, "has anyone ever told you that you are . . . uh . . . intense?"

The younger man's forehead wrinkled. "Yes."

"Well, they're right; you are. So lighten up." Henry blinked. Then blinked again. It made Jones laugh. "So serious . . . ," he scolded playfully. Then, sobering, he said, "Tell me what you have said to the people whom you have approached."

"Well . . . let's see . . . starting with my wife—and with all of them—I told them I had made a lot of mistakes. I told them I was sorry—"

Jones held a hand up. "Go no further, young man. I see the problem immediately."

"What?" Henry asked in disbelief. "What could possibly be wrong with that?"

Jones thought for a minute, then asked, "Have you ever seen a public figure—a politician or a CEO or even a movie star—embroiled in a scandal, who says, 'I made a mistake, and I'm sorry'?"

Henry nodded slowly. "Sure."

"As the scandal plays out over months—and sometimes even years after the scandal has passed—have you noticed how many people never seem to get over it, even when that celebrity says, in effect, 'Holy cow! How many times do I have to admit I made a mistake?! I'm sorry!'?"

"Yes."

"Well," Jones said, shifting his weight and propping an elbow on the suitcase beside him, "the answer is that, no, we can't just get over it, because *you*, Mr. Public Figure, evidently did not understand what you really did in the first place. You did *not* make a mistake! And therein lies the problem."

Henry was concentrating as hard as he could, but still had to admit, "I'm lost here. I'm sorry, but can you explain what you mean?"

"If one makes a mistake," Jones began, "then an apology is usually sufficient to get things back on an even keel. However— and this is a big 'however'—most people do not ever know why their apology did not seem to have any effect. It is simply that they did not make a mistake; they made a *choice* . . . and never understood the difference between the two."

"Tell me," Henry said.

"All right. Think of it this way: If you are lost, wandering through a forest in the dark, unable to see, unaware that a cliff is nearby, and you stumble off the cliff and break your neck, *that*," Jones said, with a confident toss of his head, "is a mistake.

"But let's say it's broad daylight. You are meandering about in a forest you've been told never to enter. There are No

Trespassing signs everywhere, but you think you can slip in and slip out and not get caught. Now, again let's say you fall off a cliff and break your neck . . . *that*, my friend, was not a mistake. It was a conscious choice."

"You're saying I made choices, not mistakes?" Henry asked grimly, more of a statement, really, than a question.

Jones nodded. "In most cases, I believe so. You must judge the difference of each incident on its own merit. You weren't home for your wife's birthday? That was a choice. You shorted your crew's pay? Choice. You bury irrigation lines too shallow, and they begin to appear on top of the ground after a month, because you were in too much of a hurry to do the job right? That was not a mistake. It was a choice, and the person for whom you were doing the work does not view you as unlucky or even incompetent. To him, you are dishonest. Do you understand the difference?"

With a sick expression on his face, Henry replied, "Unfortunately, yes."

"Good," said Jones, clapping his hands together. "Now you need to learn the difference in how each situation must be handled. When one simply makes a mistake, an apology—an 'I'm sorry'—will usually handle the situation. But when a *choice* has been identified, the only way to repair a relationship is by exhibiting true remorse and seeking forgiveness. Now, in some cases, where money or property might have been involved, you should also offer restitution, but showing real remorse and actually asking the question, 'Will you please forgive me?' is the only pathway to a new beginning in your business or personal life."

"I should even ask my employees to forgive me, shouldn't I?" Henry asked. He already knew the answer, but he was struggling with the lesson he had just learned—one he knew had the power to change his life . . . if he would let it.

"Without a doubt," confirmed Jones. "Many employers mistakenly believe that admitting wrongdoing and asking forgiveness from their subordinates—even for wrong personal choices that didn't directly affect the subordinates—will strip them of their ability to lead, or weaken them in the eyes of others. Quite the opposite is true. In fact, the very thing the boss fears—loss of leadership—is most often brought about because the leader did not settle the issue sufficiently in the minds of his followers by showing genuine regret and asking for forgiveness."

"And while I am thinking about it," Jones said, "asking for forgiveness must never include a phrase such as 'If I have offended you . . .' or 'If I was wrong . . .' A person experiencing true remorse *knows* he has offended and *knows* he was wrong. And the people in position to grant forgiveness can spot insincerity a mile away. Better to say nothing at all than to compound your trouble by lying about how you feel."

"You know," Henry said, "somehow I think I'll have an easier time making things right with my employees than with my wife."

Jones shrugged. "Your wife is more important. It *will* be a longer process with her. The longer you've known someone—

the more history there is between you—the longer it will take to establish in their mind that you have truly changed. Remember, forgiveness is an altogether different thing from trust or respect. Forgiveness is about the past. Trust and respect are about the future. Forgiveness will be in the hands of others and can be given to you, but trust and respect are in your own hands...and must be earned. You can do that, son, by proving to your wife that you can once again be the man she fell in love with."

Jones changed the subject abruptly. "Young man, what is the name of your unborn child?"

Henry was concentrating so hard on what Jones had been saying that he shook his head as if to clear it. He smiled and said, "My wife wants to name him Caleb. But I might go home and argue for Jones."

The old man laughed and raised both hands in the air. "No! Don't do that to a beautiful baby. Caleb is good. Do you know much about the original Caleb?"

"No, I don't."

"The original Caleb lived his life with an honorable heart and became a 'victorious old man.' Look him up sometime . . . I think you'll be interested." Jones reached out and placed his hand on Henry's head. Smiling, he closed his eyes and said, "Henry Warren . . . your son Caleb will lead a long and fruitful life. He will live his days leading others to long and fruitful lives of their own. Caleb will love his mother and father and honor and respect them. He will protect his mother and be proud of his father.

"Caleb's mother will caress him, imbue him with hope and confidence, and show him the kind of love that only a mother can—and that affection will mean the world to him. But it is Caleb's *father* who will lead him with the very example of his own life. Caleb will watch his father closely and duplicate everything his father does. Caleb will become what his father becomes."

Jones watched as tears began to stream down Henry's face. "Wow," Henry said in a voice choked with emotion. "That's pretty scary. Caleb will become what *I* become?"

"Yes," Jones replied. "Aren't you very much like your own father?"

"More than I'd like to be, I'm afraid."

"I'm sure your father did the best he knew, but he also expected you to add wisdom and understanding to what he was able to impart. You can remove the generational curses from Caleb's life by removing these impediments right now, in your own life. At this *very moment*, you possess the power of perspective. You can choose to see your life becoming whatever you wish. If you so choose, you can move the mountains in your life's path with the eventual help of those who will come to love you and learn to respect you for what you are becoming.

"But know this: you have yet to deal with the consequences of some of your actions. It will not be an easy process. There are those who will doubt your motives and warn others away from you because of your past. But let me make you a promise: if you will only face these consequences honorably and generously, seeking forgiveness with a spirit of honest remorse, you will eventually win the hearts of even those who hate you.

"Even in the midst of mighty struggle, never forget that you are Caleb's champion . . . his standard bearer . . . his rock . . . his lighthouse . . . his guide to fulfilling the promise of his namesake—a victorious old man."

Henry thought for a moment, brows knit as he stared at the ground. Then, "I can do that," he said, with a decisiveness that said he meant business. He raised his eyes to Jones. "I can do that."

Jones drilled him with a piercing gaze, as if trying to gauge the younger man's sincerity. Henry's statement registered as true. Satisfied, Jones gave a brisk nod, got to his feet, and extended his hand to Henry, who took it and stood, facing Jones. For the briefest of moments, Henry just stood there, awkwardly, but then suddenly, he wrapped the old man in a bear hug. "I'll never forget you," he said, choking back a sob.

As Jones walked toward the road, suitcase in hand, Henry Warren bowed his head and prayed for the first time since he was a boy. He asked for strength, for courage, for wisdom and understanding. He promised that, from this day forward, he would be a good husband and, soon, a good father. He also pledged to be a good boss and a true and loyal friend.

And he said thank you for an old man named Jones.

Chapter 9

"HI, YOU TWO!"

The bells on the door of the Orange Beach Pack N' Mail jangled loudly as I entered. Pack N' Mail is one of the more interesting shops in our area. In addition to the usual packing and mailing services, the eclectic little shop carries books, gifts, puzzles, and candy for any kid who happens to wander in—this in addition to being the local purveyor of Seadog T-shirts (a large part of my at-home wardrobe), which feature a pirate Dalmatian, complete with a peg leg and a patch on one eye.

Pack N' Mail is also our own modern-day version of Floyd's Barber Shop. With Café Beignet, the coffee house, next door and Mark the UPS man in and out several times a day, its employees pretty much have the scoop on what's happening in and around the Orange Beach area. Ted, the owner, is a graying middle-aged man with wire-framed glasses and a bright personality. Lynn is his younger, chestnut-haired right hand. They are among this area's favorite people. Their heads shot up at my jovial greeting.

"Hi, Andy!" both said at once.

"Can we help you with anything?" Ted asked. "Or are you here to shoot the breeze?"

"Breeze shooting," I answered with a grin. "On my way to lunch and just stopping by to say hello."

"Chinese?"

"Mm-hmm," I answered. "You hungry?"

"Yep, but too busy to eat. I saw Jones go by the front window a few minutes ago, though. Maybe you could catch him. He's your buddy, isn't he?"

"I like to think so," I replied. "I owe him more than I could ever repay. Which way was he walking?"

Ted pointed to his right. "Toward Jenny's."

The China Dragon is a local favorite for lunch. It is owned and operated by a young Asian woman who speaks very little English. Her name, written formally, might start with an X or S or Z or G, for all we know, but when she pronounces it, we all agree that it sounds something like "Jenny." So that is what we call her . . . and we call her restaurant "Jenny's."

Jenny takes orders and delivers food, runs the register, cleans and sets tables, refills drinks—and does it all with a remote phone tucked between her shoulder and ear, taking calls for carry-out. For all we know, Jenny cooks too, since no one has ever seen whoever it is she yells at in the kitchen! In fact, her only help in the restaurant is a soft-spoken young Mexican named Abraham. Everyone loves Abraham, and he often sits at the table and talks with us while we eat. Abraham's name, too, provides a source of amusement here in this small Southern community and allows us all to feel a bit more liberal than we probably are. Where else, the joke goes, can a redneck eat Chinese food, hanging out with a Mexican who has a Jewish name?

Opening the restaurant door at lunchtime afforded me the usual sight. It was packed with people of all sorts, from construction crews to businesspeople, surfers to retirees. And of course, right in the middle of it all, with the phone to her ear, was Jenny. She waved at me and pointed to the first booth on the right, just inside the door. It was the booth right beside me, actually, but I had come from the bright sunshine into the dim light of the restaurant and had not seen the old man who was so close he could have pinched me. And he did.

I jumped as he laughed. "Jones!" I exclaimed.

He stood up and hugged me. "I thought I might find you here," he said.

I was getting used to it, but it still seemed very strange to me when he said things like that and showed up the way he did. After all, I had driven away from my house not fifteen minutes earlier, unsure myself where I would eat that day. It wasn't the first time I had asked, but still, as we sat down, I *had* to try again. "Jones? How could you have possibly known you would find me here?"

He shrugged. "I just came in and sat down. A few minutes later . . . here you were." He chuckled at the look on my face.

I ordered the vegetable fried rice with wonton soup. Jones chose the beef teriyaki. As we sipped our Cokes, we talked about my family and my latest speaking engagement. It had been for several thousand businesspeople, and Jones seemed surprised when I mentioned that I had told them about him.

"I'm not sure that was a very interesting subject," he said with a wry face.

Before I could reply, Jenny approached the booth and sank to her knees beside Jones. I watched with some confusion as she took his left hand in both of hers. Quietly, briefly, amid the cacophony of the busy restaurant, she spoke to him in her native tongue, as Jones leaned close, nodding several times. Finally, Jenny stood and bowed. Haltingly, she said, "Is honor I not forget ever . . . to meet you, Chen." She bowed again and went back to her work.

It was an odd moment. Jones looked across the table at me with those amazing eyes, but I was unable to read their expression. Tenderness, love, a peaceful calm, to be sure, but was I also seeing sadness? I hoped not. I was in awe of this old man, I knew, and I was fiercely protective of him. "Are you all right?" I asked, not knowing what else to say.

"Yes," he responded with a gentle smile. "I am fine. Very fine."

I hesitated, while Jones went back to his food, but finally, I could stand it no longer. "Did you understand what Jenny was saying?"

The old man looked up with that same expression I had noticed moments before. "Yes," he said and held my gaze.

"Did she just call you 'Chen'?"

"She did."

I looked at him carefully before I asked the next question. And when I did, he appeared to be expecting it. "If Abraham were to call you by name . . . might he call you Garcia?"

He slowly nodded. "Most likely he would."

Suddenly, I felt as though I could not breathe. The familiar face in front of me was motionless, but changing—moving— *and yet it was not!* This old-man face that had caused me in the past to casually wonder whether it was of Anglo or African descent shifted visibly before me. Or was it, as he himself had said so many times, only my perception? I felt certain that, yes, the old man's face was different—and yet it never *actually* changed or moved. As I thought of him as "Garcia," he appeared quite obviously Hispanic, yet when "Chen" came to my mind, there was an old Asian man before me.

Even as I write these words now, I find that point in time almost impossible to describe. It was one of the strangest moments of my life, but still, a glimpse of greater understanding. But then, Jones gestured toward my plate, and the moment was over. "Eat," he said. "Finish. We have somewhere to go."

No longer hungry, I took a couple of bites and pronounced myself full. Leaving the money for the food on the table, I followed Jones as he picked up the ever-present suitcase, slipped out the door, and headed directly for my car. "Where are we going?" I asked, hurrying to keep up.

"Beach road," he replied, "and head west."

While I drove, Jones slept. At least I think he did. His eyes were closed, and he didn't talk, but I did as he had asked—I was driving west on the beach road—and kept quiet. I had driven for about ten minutes when, without warning, he opened his eyes and said, "Turn here."

I did, seeing immediately that we were back at the site of our first meeting, the Gulf State Park Pier, which was recently closed for repairs from storm damage. The parking lot, covered in sand, was empty.

As I slowed the car to a stop, Jones turned to look at me, pausing as if he were trying to remember something, but he never said a word. He got out of the car and began walking across the lot, then the beach, toward the familiar part of the pier where the concrete meets the sand. I followed, not knowing whether or not I was supposed to, but thinking that he had not told me to stay . . .

Jones waited for me at the edge of the pier as, again, he searched my face, but did not say anything. Then I heard it. Interrupting the sounds of the nearby seagulls and crashing waves was a distinct and sorrowful cry. It emanated from under the structure, from that hollowed-out place in the sand, a place that still appears to me sometimes in my own dreams. In the humidity and heat of midday, I had chills.

As Jones ducked under the structure, I followed nervously as the insane thought occurred to me, *Am I stepping into my past?* As my eyes adjusted to the deep shadows, I saw that it was nothing quite so dramatic. It was, however, uncomfortably familiar.

I saw a young man in shorts and a T-shirt, barefoot and sitting cross-legged, with his head buried in his hands. He was crying his heart out. It was a hopeless wail that was so reminiscent of my own desperation in this very place so long ago, that for a moment, I was almost physically ill.

The boy must have heard us, because he looked up. He was so startled that, for a second, I thought he might run—or attack us—but Jones, in between the boy and me, held out his hand. And the young man took it.

"Come here, son," Jones said. "Move into the light."

I remembered. Those were the exact words the old man had used with me almost three decades ago. *Move into the light.* I had assumed a different meaning then and wondered if this young man had really heard what had just been spoken into his life.

He shuffled forward with a sob, coughed loudly, and wiped his nose quickly with his arm. His dark hair was long and messy, but clean. *Showers at the hotel pools*, I thought. He was nineteen or twenty, thin and hard as a rail, and even in the dimness of our surroundings, I could see the effects of the sun on his skin.

"You crying about something in particular?" Jones asked.

Ignoring the question, the boy sniffed and asked, "Am I being arrested?"

Jones turned toward me and said, "That's about as silly as 'Are you going to rob me?'" Then, turning back to the young man, he asked him, "Other than the drinks in that ice chest behind you and a little moonlight trespassing, is there anything you should be arrested for?"

The boy shook his head.

"Okay then . . . Jason," Jones said meaningfully. "You don't have to worry about me. I'm old anyway. Don't you think you could take me?" The old man held his hands out and sort of juked back and forth quickly, as if he were a boxer.

The boy grinned at the old man, in spite of himself, but just as quickly, the smile was gone. "How did you know my name?" he demanded. "Who are you?"

"My name is Jones. No 'Mr.' Just plain Jones. This is Andy." He indicated me with a glance over his shoulder.

"How did you know my name?"

"No big deal, really," Jones said. "I've been watching you for a long time."

That was the same thing he had said to me . . .

"Young man," Jones went on, oblivious of my thoughts, "if you'll pull us some Cokes from your stash back there, we'll get started."

Jason didn't move. "Get started doing what?" he asked in a challenging voice.

"We need to start noticing a few things," Jones answered. "We need to check your heart. We need to gather a little perspective."

Still wary, the young man said, "I don't know what you're talking about . . ."

Jones looked around at me and winked, then said to Jason, "I am a noticer. It is my gift. While others may be able to sing well or run fast, I notice things that other people overlook. And you know, most of them are in plain sight." The old man cocked his head. "I notice things about situations and people that produce perspective. That's what most folks lack—perspective—a broader view. So I give 'em that broader view . . . and it allows them to regroup, take a breath, and begin their lives again."

After a short staring contest between the young man and the old one, Jason withdrew into the darkness and came back with three soft drinks. One he kept, the second he handed to Jones, and the third he fired at me with a backhand flip. I caught the can and I caught his eye. He had thrown it way harder than he had needed to. *No shortage of aggression there*, I mused, *and a whole lot of anger. Oh well, I know how you feel, kid.* I knew Jones had not missed the shot, but he didn't say anything.

"Thanks for the Coke," the old man said; then he turned to me and remarked slyly, "Your reflexes seem to be good."

I was still trying to keep from throwing the Coke back at the kid. Instead, I just nodded and gave Jones a tight smile.

Jones said to the young man, "So . . . no family, huh?"

"How do you know that?"

Jones shrugged as if to say, *Everyone knows*, but when Jason glanced at me, I knew that he and I *both* knew that everyone didn't.

"Dead . . . split . . . one or the other," Jason said. "Either way, no matter."

Jones thought about that answer, then nodded and said, "As far as how you feel right now, I am sorry, but in regards to your future . . . you're right. No matter."

The old man's answer seemed to make Jason angrier. "What is *that* supposed to mean?"

"Oh, nothing," Jones said with false innocence. "I was just agreeing with you. No matter your past . . . you can choose your future. I thought that's what *you* meant."

Jason was silent, but I almost laughed out loud. The old man had trapped him, and he knew it. But just as I had done in his place, the young man took one more stab at stating his case. "Look. I'm kind of hopeless, okay? It's obvious that my life is getting worse and worse. So let's just leave it at that, all right?"

Jones shook his head. "Well, no," he said. "Sorry, but I don't think I *can* leave it just like that."

"What?" Jason said in a surly manner that was fast making me as aggravated as he was.

Jones evidently noticed it too. "Actually," the old man said with a reproving smile, "'Sir?' rather than 'What?' might have been a more appropriate response . . . but we'll get into that later. For now, let me concentrate on this: You said that your life was getting worse and worse. While I believe that was just an off-hand comment, I want you to know and understand that, unfortunately, it is an actual fact."

"What is a fact?" the young man asked.

Jones answered, "That your life *really* is getting worse and worse. And in measurable ways. Physically, financially, and emotionally, your life is getting worse and worse."

"I don't believe that," Jason sneered.

"Really?" Jones said in mock disbelief. "So *you* say it and it's true; I say it and it's *not* true?"

Jason didn't know how to respond to that, so he said nothing. I have to admit, Jones was exhibiting a lot more patience with this kid than I was feeling. But I knew where he was going with this "worse and worse" bit.

Jones took a deep breath. "Young man," he said to Jason, "do you agree that opportunities and encouragement come from people?"

Jason didn't answer immediately, but finally said, "I'm not sure what you mean."

The old man restated his question. "Do you agree that life's opportunities for advancement and financial achievement come from people? That verbal or written encouragement comes from people? True, specific people are placed in your life for a particular reason, but in general, *people* are the delivery vehicle for opportunity and encouragement. Correct?"

"I guess . . ."

"No guessing," Jones said firmly. "Do you agree that life's opportunities and encouragement come from people? Yes or no?"

"Yes."

"Excellent," Jones responded. "Now, I want you to make a connection. If it is true that your life is getting worse and worse, could that be because you are receiving fewer opportunities and encouragement than you could use?"

"Yeah, I guess . . . I mean, that could be true."

"So, knowing that your opportunities and encouragement

come from people, why are you not getting your share of opportunities and encouragement?"

Jason stared for a moment, then said, "I don't know. You tell me."

"All right," Jones said, "I will. You are not receiving opportunities and encouragement that people have to share for a very simple reason. No one wants to be around you."

At that, I readied myself to dive in front of Jones and protect him from the attack that I was certain was about to take place. Instead, the young man closed his lips tightly, cast his eyes down for a few seconds, then back up to meet the old man's gaze. "Okay. I can believe that." The next thing out of his mouth astounded me. "So what do I do about it?"

"Before I explain what you can do about it," Jones replied, "you must understand the opposite dynamic. There are, as you might have guessed, people whose lives are getting better and better. Do you know anyone like that?"

Jason was listening intently. So was I.

"Do you know someone," Jones continued, "whose life in every way just seems to work? He has opportunities one after another and seems never to get discouraged? Well, there *are* people like that. So, if opportunities and encouragement come from other people, and one of these special achievers seems to be getting more than his fair share of opportunities and encouragement from them, why might that be?"

Without pausing, Jones gave us the answer. "I'll tell you why: it's because that person who seems to have the Midas touch has become someone that others want to be around! That person is fun, happy, and exciting. He is a 'people magnet,' and when there are opportunities to be shared and encouragement to be given, this person gets more than, for instance, *you*."

Once again, I was ready for Jason to lash out—perhaps even physically—but once again, he surprised me. "I can see that," he said. "But what can I do?"

"It's very simple," Jones answered. "Young man, you must become a person that others want to be around! This is far and away the greatest success secret in existence. A man or woman who has become someone others want to be around holds the world by the tail. He can get a meeting with any executive. Why? Because he is loved and appreciated by the executive's assistant! *He* gets the listing, gets the sale or the promotion. He gets the extra help, the extra time, and the pay. He gets the chance, the second chance, and the benefit of the doubt. And all because people like him."

"I don't mean to be dense," Jason said, "but how do I become this person? I really do believe you—even though I still don't know why you're here—but how do I do it? How do I change? How do I know *what* to change?"

Jones leaned forward. So did I. I didn't want to miss a word of what was coming next. Jones was about to reveal to the young man the same wisdom he had once given me—the simple instruction that had shaped my life! "Jason," he said intently, "I believe you should ask yourself every day, 'What is it about *me* that other people would change if they could?' This is incredibly important introspection. What is it about *you*, Jason, that other people would change if they could?"

The young man repeated it to Jones. "What is it about *me* that other people would change if they could?" He wrinkled his brow, then asked, "What if I get an answer . . . and I don't want to change that thing?"

Jones laughed. "In that case, you'll just have to remember . . . that wasn't the question! The question was, 'What would *other* people change about me if they could?'" The old man quickly grew serious. "See, if you ever want folks to believe in you, then it really helps if they like you.

"So, check yourself in as many areas as you can dream up. What is it about the way I *dress* that other people would change if they could? What is it about the way I *act* that other people would change if they could? What is it about the way I *talk* that other people would change if they could? And on and on. See what I mean?"

"I do," Jason said. "About the 'talking' part . . . why did you say a few minutes ago that 'Sir' would have been a better choice?"

"Well," Jones began, "the answer 'yes' and 'yes sir' are both *correct* responses. Likewise 'no' and 'no sir.' 'Yes' and 'yes ma'am' . . . 'no' and 'no ma'am' the same. Got it?"

"I do."

"Here's the only difference . . . and where you need to make a choice. Studies have shown that to the majority of people, it makes no difference at all which way you answer. But there is a significant percentage—for the sake of argument, let's say 20 percent—who feel that adding the 'sir' or the 'ma'am' is *much* more respectful.

"Here's my point. If you are endeavoring to become a person that other people want to be around, don't you want to include that 20 percent in your corner? That's just one example, mind you.

"Here's another. There are people who don't mind the occasional curse word sprinkled into a conversation; there are also folks who don't want to hear *any* curse words. Now, *you* may not think there is anything wrong with cursing, but if you want to become a person that others want to be around, you must always hold your life to the very highest standard."

Jason smiled. "I get it. I mean, I really understand this."

"Of course you do," the old man said. "And, Jason, you have an incredible future ahead of you. One day, you will look back on this 'worst time' in your life as a fortuitous event. Even your worst times have value and can become, in retrospect, your best times. Know, Jason, that you are destined to make a difference in the world. Do you understand what I am saying?"

"I . . . I think so," the young man said sincerely. "And . . . and I want to make a difference."

"Oh, you *will* make a difference," Jones said, nodding. "Now, what *kind* of difference? That, my young friend, is entirely up to you. As for me?"—Jones winked—"I am expecting the difference you make to be a great one!" And with that, Jones reached out to shake the young man's hand. "I'll be leaving you now," he said as he opened his old suitcase away from me, "but I have something for you." Jones paused, then asked, "Do you read?"

"Yeah," Jason said. Then he grinned widely. "I mean, yes *sir*, I do."

Jones smiled. "Okay then," Jones murmured softly as he brought from the suitcase three small, orange hardcover books. I strained to see if they were the same titles I remembered. And they were. More worn perhaps, but they seemed to be the very same books. *Winston Churchill. Will Rogers. George Washington Carver.*

As I crawled out from under that pier a few minutes later, my emotions were as raw and on edge as any time I can remember. I wanted to tell the kid how lucky he was to have had that time with Jones. I wanted to tell him how his life could turn out, if only he would work and believe. And I must admit, I would have paid any price for those three books at that moment—I wanted them on the corner of *my* desk, in *my* office—but I determined that they were infinitely more valuable in the hands and mind and heart of *another* young man.

As for Jones, when I straightened up and turned around, he was not behind me. I listened carefully to see if I could hear his voice, thinking he must have gone back to tell the boy something he had forgotten. But after a time, I walked around to the other side of the pier. Was he, I wondered, waiting for me there? He wasn't. I shook my head and grinned, then laughed aloud as I walked back to my car. I assumed that I would run into the old man in a few days or a week. He would show up again, I figured, where and when I least expected.

It wasn't until the following morning when I knew . . . this time, my friend was truly gone.

Chapter 10

THE PHONE RANG AT 8:14 A.M. HAVING WORKED UNTIL the wee hours of the morning, I was still asleep, but my wife had been up and dealing with the boys for a while. She got it on the second ring, and before I could drift back into unconsciousness, Polly was at my side, with the phone in her hand.

"Dear?" She shook me gently.

"Hey," I mumbled, rolling over and forcing my eyes open.

Polly shook me again. "Wake up, dear," she said. "It's Ted from Pack N' Mail. He seems upset and says he needs to talk to you now."

I frowned, still trying to clear my head. "What time is it?" I asked.

"Eight fifteen."

"Okay."

Polly handed me the phone but stayed beside me. I propped myself on one elbow and watched my wife's face as I answered. "Hi, Ted."

"Hi, Andy," he said. "I'm sorry to bother you . . ."

"You're not bothering me. What's up?"

"Well," he began, "I didn't know who else to call . . . I didn't want to call the police . . ."

He had my attention now. I was fully awake. Sitting up, I asked, "Ted, what's wrong?"

"It may be nothing . . ." he said.

"Ted!"

"I found Jones's suitcase in the parking lot this morning. By itself. Right out in the *middle* of the parking lot. And he is nowhere around."

Well, I didn't know what to say to that. A million things ran through my mind at once. Was the old man hurt? Had he forgotten it? Had it been stolen from him and left there? Was Ted certain it was Jones's suitcase?

"Did you take it inside?" I asked.

"No," Ted answered hesitantly. "None of the businesses are open here yet, so there aren't many cars. I . . . I just didn't want to move it. Should I?"

"Maybe not," I answered. "Hang on. I'll be right there."

Quickly, I told Polly what I knew as I slipped into a T-shirt and one of my Tommy Bahama swimsuits that pass for shorts in our beach town. I brushed my teeth, kissed Polly and the boys, and was in the car within five minutes.

I made the short drive up the beach in another seven or eight minutes and pulled into the parking lot to see a small crowd gathered around the suitcase. Ted was right. There were very few cars. It was mostly the people who had come to work early.

I drove right up to the group and got out. Ted stood by the suitcase. Susan and Clay were there from the Winn-Dixie across the parking lot. Jenny and Abraham were standing with Al from the coffee shop. They all stared at me as I approached, no one talking; no one even said hello.

I stopped at Ted and looked at him for a moment—expecting him to do what, I wasn't sure—but he seemed to be in a daze. I knelt down beside the suitcase. "Has anyone touched it?" I asked.

"No, no," they all answered. No one had.

I understood. I didn't want to touch it either. Strange, really . . . We had all seen the suitcase many times. We had engaged in conversations about it. We had curiously noticed how careful Jones had always been to never let anyone carry it for him or peek inside as he opened it. Yet, here it was, right in front of us, and not a soul wanted to be the first to touch it.

The suitcase was battered yet smooth—in the way only a truly old object can be. Its surface had been a dark brown once, but all the original color was long gone, leaving a deep tan. It was ribboned with tiny crevices and reminded me of the old man's skin . . . soft and stout at the same time, durable, with dimension and character that seemed to grow more obvious with age.

Slowly, I placed my hand on it, left it there for a moment, then removed it. Looking up, I saw that several others had quietly joined the group. Tom and Becky from the pharmacy, several of the girls from the nail salon, and a couple of guys from the tackle store had come to watch or wait or whatever it was we were doing. Word was spreading. Looking up, I asked, "Should we take it inside?" and everyone agreed that, yes, we should.

I stood and looked again at Ted. "You," he said simply and stepped back.

So I picked up the old man's suitcase. It was surprisingly light, though not empty, I didn't think. As a group—and there were almost twenty of us now—we walked across the parking lot and into Café Beignet. I took the suitcase to a table in the center of the room and laid it carefully on its side. Everyone from the parking lot had come into the coffee shop, and they just kind of stood there until Al began pouring coffee. Soon, we all settled uneasily into chairs at several tables, loosely arranged around the suitcase.

"We have neighbors that were divorcing," Clay said to no one in particular, "until they met Jones." We all looked at him. He looked back, then shrugged. "Just thought I'd tell you," he said.

"Is he all right?" Susan asked, directing her question to me. "I mean, he's not hurt somewhere, is he?"

"I don't know," I answered honestly. "I hope not . . . and I don't really think so. You guys all know how Jones is. He's in and out.

No pattern to where he goes or when." I paused, then added, "I've just never known him to be without this thing." We all stared at the battered old suitcase, now sitting center stage in what was fast becoming a mystery none of us wanted any part of.

We looked up as the door opened and several more people came in, including Robert Craft and Barry and Jan Hanson. Robert pulled a chair up and sat next to me. "I heard," he said, then asked quietly, "Any word?" I shook my head.

Al began to distribute big plates of beignets on all the tables and pour coffee for the newcomers. And every few minutes, more would arrive. John and Shannon Smith, Mike and Melanie Martin, Jonathan and Debra Langston, Alan and Karen McBride, the Granthams, the Millers, the Norwoods, all the Wards, all the Kaisers . . . and those were just the people I knew. Folks sipped coffee nervously, but I noticed that, as good as those beignets smelled, there didn't seem to be much of an appetite for them.

"Hey, everybody?" I asked as something occurred to me. "I'm just curious . . . does anyone have any idea where Jones sleeps at night? Where he stays? Has he ever spent a night with any of you?" Blank stares. "Oh well," I sighed. "It was a thought . . ."

"You know," Ted said, "I'd go look for him if I had the slightest clue where to start."

"Well," said Alan, "he's certainly disappeared before. Haven't there been times we haven't seen him for a while?" We all just looked at him. He bobbed one shoulder, uneasily. "Yeah, I know," he said. "Never without the suitcase."

Since I had laid it on the table, I had not touched it again, and no one else had either.

The door opened again, and I saw Jason, the kid from the pier, come in with a couple of the boat captains from the marina. I nodded at him, and he self-consciously gave me a half wave in return.

"I don't suppose anyone knows where he's from . . ." someone threw out.

No one did.

"My life was about to end when I met Jones," Jake Conner said. "I don't think it is any secret that I was going bankrupt."

All heads turned toward the back of the room. Jake Conner? Bankrupt? Well, it was a secret to me. And if the faces around the room could be read, it was a secret to a lot of us. Jake was one of the richest men in the area. And one of the meanest, too, if I am to believe all the stories. But according to local legend, he had changed overnight several years earlier, and no one knew why. Now, it appeared, we were about to hear how it happened.

Jake began to talk. "I've never told anyone this before, but when I said, 'My life was about to end,' that was not entirely accurate. The truth is, I was about to end my life. Some notes came due at the same time the stock market went south. Financially, I was turned inside out. Anyway, I was embarrassed. I was . . . scared. So I slipped the *Mistee Linn* out of the marina and through the pass about dark one evening." The *Mistee Linn*, we all knew, was the eighty-seven-foot yacht that Jake kept in Terry Cove.

"I stood on the flying bridge for a couple of hours, thinking, feeling sorry for myself while trying to drum up my courage for what I was about to do. My intention was to set the autopilot on 180—due south—and just slip overboard. Somebody would've found the boat when she ran out of fuel, and the insurance companies would have paid my family quickly. Nobody could have proven suicide and . . . well . . ." Jake's voice drifted to silence. His eyes were fixed on a spot in his memory that none of us could see—that none of us *wanted* to see.

Roger Kaiser broke the spell. "But you're here, Jake," he said quietly. "Why didn't you do it?"

Jake turned to Roger and smiled oddly, as if he himself did not believe what he was about to say. "I didn't do it," he said, "because Jones tapped me on the shoulder and told me not to." Jake let that sink in, then added, "My wife nearly collected that insurance money anyway. I thought I was going to have a heart attack right there.

"Here's the thing . . . I know—I mean, I *know*—that old man was *not* on that boat when I left the dock. He was not. He was just . . . not. I've thought about it ten million times since that night. I was suicidal, not *crazy*, and I'm telling each and every one of you, I was alone when I went out the pass."

"It's a big boat, Jake," Roger said skeptically. "Lots of rooms . . ."

Jake sighed deeply. "Okay. Fine. You believe what you want to . . . But the part I meant to tell anyway was about Jones talking to me for hours that night. And on into the next morning. When we got through, my debts were still there, but I had a new look at the whole thing—a new 'perspective,' he called it. And I managed to pull it all together. Everybody got paid. And I think *I'm* a new man. In any case, I never saw him again until he showed up here—what was it now?—six, seven weeks ago?"

I did quick calculations in my head. Yes, it had only been a few weeks since Jones had come to town.

"You all knew my Harrison . . ."

All heads swung to a voice near the bookcase on the side wall. It belonged to Nancy Carpenter, a lady in her early sixties. I knew her from the bank, where she was a teller, and by the volunteer work in which she was always involved. Her husband, Harrison, had been the probate judge and had died several years ago after a long bout with lung cancer. Yes, I assumed, most of us in the room had known Harrison Carpenter.

Nancy stood up. "Harrison died three years ago—well, next month'll make three years." Her voice broke, and she took a moment to compose herself. "As I look around this morning," she said finally, "I see quite a few of you who were at Harrison's wake. No one has ever asked me about it—out of courtesy, I suppose—but I know many of you must have wondered why Harrison was buried with a dinner fork in his hand. But maybe you didn't even notice it . . ."

Notice it? Was she kidding? It was the only thing the town talked about for a month! And every time any mention of a funeral came up during the last three years, someone was bound to say, "Remember the guy lying in the casket with a fork in his hand?" But Nancy was correct: we never asked. We liked Harrison, we loved her, and it just didn't seem appropriate to bring it up. But boy, were we listening now!

"Like Jake," she said, shooting him a quick glance, "I never told anyone this before." She took a deep breath. "You know, Harrison was having a tough time several months before he . . . uh . . . before he passed away. Not physically so much, though that was hard. We slept in different rooms. We had not done that in thirty-eight years of marriage, but the medicine kept him awake, and he coughed all the time, so we slept in separate rooms . . ." She stopped for a beat, lost in thought and memories swirling around in her head. But then, quite suddenly, she snapped out of her reverie. "What was I saying? Oh. He was having a hard time. He had no peace about dying. Of course, *I* didn't. I mean, how *can* you, really? we thought. He got to the point where he cried a lot and just never got out of bed. I cried a lot too.

"Anyway, several weeks before Harrison died, I woke up in the middle of the night and heard Harrison laughing. And I heard *another* voice in that room." Nancy paused. "Where Harrison was," she added.

"At first, I thought he had the television on, but after a few minutes, I went to see for myself." Then Nancy's chin lifted a bit, as if she was about to make some sort of declaration that she dared us to dispute. "I peeked around the corner, into the room, and Jones was in there with him. I didn't know him as Jones at that time, of course. To me, he was just some old man who had gotten in the house. I was horrified.

"I ran immediately to check the doors, but they were still locked, still *chained*. I tried to call the police, but the phone wouldn't work. I tried my cell phone, and it wouldn't work either. Then I thought, well, maybe Harrison let him in. I mean, he hadn't gotten out of bed in days, so I didn't *really* think so, but . . ." She shrugged.

Everyone in the coffee shop was silent and absolutely still. The only movement in the room was a steady stream of people squeezing themselves in the front door as Nancy talked.

"I went back to the bedroom. Jones introduced himself and said he was Harrison's best friend. Harrison said the same thing. He said this old man was his best friend, but I knew that neither of us had ever laid eyes on him. Harrison seemed calm, though . . . happy, even . . . so I sat down on the chair in the corner and listened.

"They talked and talked. Finally, Jones brought up the subject of Harrison's mother. She died before we were married, so I never met her, but I had heard lots of stories. Harrison loved his mother. Anyway, Jones said, 'Remember, Harrison? Remember how your mama used to set such a big table at Thanksgiving and Christmas?' When the old man said that, my husband closed his eyes and smiled. I had not seen him that happy in a long time, but the old man's voice just calmed him . . . soothed him.

"Then the old man—Jones—said, 'Harrison? Do you remember what your mama served? Ham, turkey, sweet potatoes, yeast rolls, peas? She cooked creamed corn and cranberry sauce and that green jello salad?' At that point, I leaned close to them," Nancy said, "because the old man was talking softer and softer. I heard him say, 'But everyone's favorite was your mama's dessert, wasn't it, Harrison? Your mama could really do dessert. Pecan pies, coconut cake, those little apple turnovers . . . and remember the sugar cookies? But it was the pumpkin pie that was your favorite. Remember?

"'Now,' the old man said, 'do you remember what your mama always said to everybody as she cleared the table? Remember, Harrison? Right before dessert? She would take the dishes away, but say, "Keep your fork . . . the best is yet to come!"'

Tears began to roll down Nancy's face. "As I said," she bravely went on, "I have never told anyone this before, but before Jones left, he kissed my husband on his head and said, 'You don't have to be afraid anymore, Harrison. You can keep your fork. The best is yet to come.'"

We were quiet, unsure how to respond when Nancy added one more thing. "I never saw Jones again either, until a few weeks ago. And it was me . . . I put the fork in Harrison's hand when he died. He had asked me to." She lifted her chin again. "And I was glad to do it. I believe the same thing now, you know . . . that the best is yet to come."

For several minutes, it seemed no one had anything to say. Then, everyone did. For almost three hours, people told story after story about Jones or Garcia or Chen or whatever name they had used for the old man. Polly slipped in while Nancy was talking and urged me to tell what Jones had meant to me and how it was that I came to know him.

Pat Simpson was there with his wife, Claudia. Pat told us about seeing Jones as a boy and how the old man had intervened one night and kept him out of trouble.

We heard several stories similar to Pat's.

Sharon Tyler's seventeen-year-old son, Brandon, had seen Jones when he was fourteen. He had been in an automobile accident with two older boys. He swore, Sharon said, that the old man he had seen around town the past few weeks was the same old man who had ridden in the ambulance with him three years earlier. Brandon had talked about the old man ever since, his mother told us, but of course, the ambulance attendants told his parents that their son had been delirious—that no one besides the paramedics had been with him at all.

Almost ten years ago, Boyd Crawford told us, he and his son pulled an old man out of Wolf Bay in the middle of the night. They were shrimping and just about ran over him with the boat. It had been Jones. They had saved him, they thought. "Turned out," Boyd said, "the old dude saved us.

"Me and my boy was buttin' heads somethin' awful. Startin' to hate each other, we was. Wadn't right; we knew it. And my wife, she cried night and day about it. We just didn't know what to do. Danged if that old joker didn't talk us out of hatin' each other—right there on the boat. I don't even remember how the man got the subject going. But by the time daylight rolled around and we was trailerin' the boat, me and the boy was huggin' and cryin' our own selves. Old dude was gone before we got in the truck. Never saw him again neither . . . until lately."

Finally, no one had any more stories to tell, or, at least, stories that they were going to share with everyone else. As I looked around, there were more than a hundred people crammed into that little coffee shop. And every one of them, it seemed, had some connection to my old friend. The more I thought about it, the more overwhelming it seemed.

To be honest, I didn't know what to make of all the stories about Jones appearing here and there or not being there when one turned around. But there was a pattern, impossible to deny, of Jones being where something special was needed—where some*one* special was needed. I could not deny it in my own life or in the lives of all the people gathered around that suitcase that morning.

I glanced around me. I knew where most of them worked. It was after 11 a.m., and most had evidently elected to delay going in. Some of them owned businesses, and those businesses, obviously, were remaining closed until they arrived. There were parents there with their children, who had not yet been taken to school.

I looked at my watch again, then across the room at Polly, with a question on my face. She cocked her head and gave a little shrug. I took a deep breath and stood. "No one in here has any way of contacting Jones," I said. "Is that right?" No one responded. "Anyone with any idea where to send this suitcase so it would reach him?" Again, nothing.

"If no one has any objections," I then said carefully, "I think we should go ahead and open it. There's no lock. We won't need to break it open. Let's see if there is anything inside that will give us a clue . . . an address . . . something."

Everyone agreed that, yes, we might as well open it—so, with not a sound in the place, I turned the suitcase and its latches toward me. No one breathed. Every person in that coffee shop heard the scratching, squeaky sound of the latches as they slid sideways and allowed the battered old suitcase to pop open a bare half inch.

When it did, a tiny, fifty-nine-cent package of seeds fell out onto the table. Necks craned and people moved as they all tried to see what had fallen out. I picked up the package, examined it briefly, and held it up for everyone else to see. It was just an ordinary paper package of seeds, no bigger than a playing card, like you've seen a million times in the garden center of any store. Marigold seeds.

While I was looking at the seeds, someone, trying to get a better view, bumped the table on which the suitcase was sitting. Through the crack in the suitcase slid two more packages almost identical to the first, except that one held tomato seeds, and the other held snapdragons.

I picked them up and passed them to Ted, who was across from me. "Go ahead. Open it up," he said. So I did.

When the top half of the battered old suitcase began to rise and pull away from the bottom half, it was apparent that there was no divider inside the ancient luggage. Seeds—brightly colored paper packages of seeds—fell everywhere. They filled the bottom half of the suitcase to overflowing, but the packages that had been stuffed into the top half fell onto the table, across the table, and onto the floor.

I quickly raked through them. Squash. Daisy. Cucumber. Forget-me-nots. Oleander. Heather. Zinnias. Okra. Watermelon. Turnip. Black-eyed Susans. Lilies. Geraniums. Pumpkin. Iris. Bellflower. And cantaloupe. It was obvious that there were at least several hundred packages—as many as the suitcase could hold—and who knew how many varieties.

Stunned and confused, we all gathered around, talking softly and shuffling haphazardly through the packages of seeds until Dave Winck pulled from the bottom of the pile a small, white envelope. We grew quiet again. With silent encouragement from us all, Dave slowly and carefully opened the envelope.

Sliding a folded piece of paper from inside, he held it for all to see, then unfolded it. "It's a note," Dave said and looked up, "and it's from him." He handed it to me and said, "You read it. Let's all hear it at the same time."

I took the paper from Dave and smiled when I heard several nervous chuckles. I wasn't the only one who noticed my hand shaking. Seeing the page first as a whole, I noticed that it was handwritten in the neat but shaky scrawl of an old man. Out loud, I began to read:

My dear friends,

For so long now I have been among you and cared for each of you more than you could possibly know. Many times, even when you did not see me or sense my presence, I was there—watching closely and listening carefully.

Your time on this earth is a gift to be used wisely. Don't squander your words or your thoughts. Consider that even the simplest actions you take for your lives matter beyond measure . . . and they matter forever.

I do not believe that you will see me again, here, in this place, but trust that the seeds I have planted in your minds and hearts will be sufficient to carry you forward. These are the seeds of perspective. During the challenging times ahead, you will find that simple seed of perspective more valuable than diamonds or gold.

It is an <u>answer</u>, of course, that most people seek in times of turmoil. Sometimes that answer is immediate, but it is not seen due to a lack of perspective. Many of you have seen this in your own lives. However, you also now know a secret that most do not understand. The reason an answer is not often found in the midst of crisis is that many times, at that very moment, a specific answer does not exist!

In desperate times, much more than anything else, folks need perspective. For perspective brings calm. Calm leads to clear thinking. Clear thinking yields new ideas. And ideas produce the bloom . . . of an answer. Keep your head and heart clear. Perspective can just as easily be lost as it can be found.

I have left these seeds for you as a simple reminder that you must also plant your own seeds in the minds and hearts of those you touch. You will honor my memory with your work.

I am not gone. I will be around. The best is yet to come.

Jones

After a bit, folks began to come forward. Most read the note again themselves and took a package or two of seeds before they left to go to work or school or home. When there were only a few of us still around, we took seeds of our own.

The suitcase is now part of an informal arrangement that allows it to be passed around a bit. Ted keeps it occasionally in Pack N' Mail so that people can see it and touch it when they visit. Then Al might keep it for a while at Café Beignet, or Ted and Kathryn at Wall Decor. I know Nancy kept it at Sea N Suds for several weeks, and Robert Craft had it in the pro shop at the golf course. I've even seen it behind the counter with Clay and Tom in the Winn-Dixie pharmacy.

As for me? Every now and then, I can't help but stare at a white-haired old man. Just hoping, I suppose. Most often, I smile when I see the stalks of corn beside a mailbox, or watermelons growing right out in someone's front yard. It is easy now to drive down almost any street in our community and see a visible reminder of what happened. People have planted the seeds that were in the suitcase, just like they've planted the ones left in their lives, which have now given birth to the certainty that, yes, when we notice things about ourselves and other people that allow us all to regroup, take a breath, and begin our lives again, the best is surely yet to come. That has been the greatest gift we received, the gift of a new perspective . . . from an old man named Jones.

The End

ACKNOWLEDGMENTS

I AM BLESSED TO BE SURROUNDED BY FRIENDS AND FAMILY who have become a team of which I am thrilled to be a part. If I can ever be perceived as a person who makes good and informed choices, it is only because of my reliance on these people's wise counsel. Thank you all for your presence in my life.

To Polly, my wife and best friend. You are beautiful, smart, and witty . . . after twenty years it is still a great combination.

To Austin and Adam, our boys. You bring me joy and perspective. I never knew I could love so much.

To Robert D. Smith, my personal manager and champion. After twenty-seven years together, you still amaze me every day.

To Scott Jeffrey, the Bear Bryant of "life coaches."

To Duane Ward and the whole incredible gang at Premiere Speaker's Bureau: You are not just partners—you are friends.

To Gail and Mike Hyatt, who gave life to my career as an author.

To Reneé, my editor, whose careful eye and quick mind made this a much better book.

To Matt Baugher, publisher; Stephanie Newton, publicist; Emily Sweeney, marketing director; Kristi Johnson, marketing specialist; and Jenn McNeil, managing editor at Thomas Nelson.

To Sandi Dorff, Paula Tebbe, and Susie White, who direct the daily parts of my life. Without the effort, prayer, and attention to detail of these three ladies, my own efforts would not come to nearly so much.

To Jared McDaniel, for his sense of humor and artistic ability.

To Nicholas Francis for his Web mastery.

To Nate Bailey for his organizational skills, happy demeanor, and "never say die" attitude.

To authors Dave Barry, Gloria Gaither, Jack Higgens, Andy Stanley, and others too numerous to mention. Your influence on my style is probably apparent, but I wanted to say "thanks" anyway. Special thanks to Gary Chapman and his amazing book *The Five Love Languages* for inspiring Jones to "notice" the animal dialects in Chapter 3!

To Katrina and Jerry Anderson, Don Brindley, Sunny Brownlee, Foncie and Joe Bullard, Brent Burns, Myrth and Cliff Callaway, Gloria and Bill Gaither, Gloria and Martin Gonzalez, Lynn and Mike Jakubik, Patsy Jones, Karen and Alan McBride, Liz and Bob McEwen, Edna McLoyd, Mary and Jim Pace, Glenda and Kevin Perkins, Brenda and Todd Rainsberger, Kathy and Dick Rollins, Shannon and John D. Smith, Claudia and Pat Simpson, Jean and Sandy Stimpson, Dr. Christopher Surek, Maryann and Jerry Tyler, Wade, Pat, Joey, and Elizabeth Ward, Mary Ann and Dave Winck, and Kathy and Mike Wooley. Your influence in my life is undeniable, and your example is very much appreciated.

A READER'S GUIDE

FOR

The

NOTICER

In this heartwarming narrative by New York Times best-selling author Andy Andrews, the sagelike instruction of Jones helps a younger version of Andy dramatically alter the course of his life—from living as a homeless person under a pier, to Andy's modern-day success. As it turns out, Andy isn't the only lost soul the mysterious Jones has impacted . . .

This Reader's Guide was created to facilitate a better understanding of what Jones calls "perspective" in The Noticer. These questions may be used for group discussion or personal reflection. It is the author's hope that the reader's understanding of perspective and the inspirational life lessons in each chapter will lead to an extraordinary life and the desire to share these lessons with others.

GENERAL QUESTIONS

1. If you could ask Jones one question, what would it be? How do you think he would respond? What advice could you give him?

2. Do you think it's easier for people to discuss their problems with people they barely know?

3. Why do you think Andy decided to title this book *The Noticer*?

4. Why did Jones prefer to be referred to as just "Jones"? Do you think this was his first or last name? Does it make a difference?

5. How can you take these ideas presented by Jones and seek out people who may need a new perspective of their own?

CHAPTER 1

1. What would happen if you asked yourself every day the same question that Jones asked Andy when they first met? ("What is it about me that other people would change if they could?") Create a list of ten things that people would change about

you if they could. Of these ten things, which one do you think they would change first?

2. In chapter 1, Jones reminds us, "Whatever you focus upon, increases." Are there areas in your life that could use some refocusing?

3. In chapter 1, Jones says, "What would you think if I told you that, yes, your bad choices and decisions have had a part in your ending up under this pier, but beyond that, under this pier is exactly where you should be in order for a future to occur that you can't even imagine at this point?" Is there a specific experience in your life that made no sense to you at the time, but now you know it was imperative that you experience it in order to be where you are today? Explain.

CHAPTER 2

1. Why does Jones avoid taking credit for Andy's success during their chance encounter at Sea N Suds? Instead of taking the credit, Jones says, "I met Andy when he was a much younger man." Is Jones responsible for Andy's success, or is Andy? Why or why not? Who's responsible for your success?

2. Is there someone important in your life who speaks a different

love "dialect" than you do? Can you think of a specific time when this concept (explained to Jan and Barry) might have been helpful in your situation?

3. How does your current perspective on life differ from Jones's views on perspective? Can you give an example or situation where a "lack of perspective" could have been avoided?

4. Jones tells us in chapter 2 that a true friend "brings out the best in you." Would you say your current friends bring out the best in you, or is it time to reevaluate the people with whom you associate?

CHAPTER 3

1. In chapter 3, Jones reveals the remaining two dialects that we use to convey love. The four dialects are *spoken words of approval, favors and deeds, physical contact,* and *love expressed in quality time.* Which dialect do you employ? Do you think it's possible for an individual to possess two different dialects, one for conveying love and one for feeling loved? Can a person learn a new dialect? Why or why not?

2. Which dialect do you think Jones uses? Give specific examples from the book to support your answer.

3. Jones makes an excellent comparison between the four dialects and four corresponding animals. Do you think there's any significant connection between pet owners, the pets they own, and the dialect with which they communicate?

CHAPTER 4

1. Walker's idea of happiness is expressed as "an elusive, moving target that seemed to perpetually flit just beyond his grasp. His thoughts were consumed by possibilities of problems and mistakes, personal slights and professional sabotage." How can a person's success be sabotaged by his or her own inability to be happy? Has there ever been a time in your life when your own inability to be happy got in the way of your success?

2. Why do you think Walker was compelled to help Jones that night, when really, it was Walker who needed the help?

3. "It's time to stop letting your history control your destiny," says Jones. He then says to Walker, "You worry because you're smart" and tells him that he is misusing his creative imagination. In what ways are you misusing your creative imagination? How can you acknowledge this way of thinking and turn it off?

4. If Jones were to ask you this question, "What are the imme-diate thoughts in your mind, say, during the first ten minutes after you wake up every morning?" how would you respond? Make a new list that refocuses your thoughts on the things in your life that you are grateful for (names, objects, feelings, etc.). How can making this list every day improve your life?

5. Do you think it was Andy's intention to give the character Walker Miles such a symbolic name? Why or why not? How is it symbolic?

CHAPTER 5

1. In what areas of your life can wisdom be helpful when mak-ing decisions? What are some ways you can acquire wisdom?

2. Why does Jones consider one's choice of friends a critical component to acquiring wisdom?

3. In chapter 5, Jones explains his concept of a leaf as an indi-cator. He says, "One can walk through the forest and never look up. But you can pick up a single leaf and know all sorts of information about the tree you are under." In what other areas of your life can this concept be applied?

CHAPTER 6

1. Self-perceptions can dictate your success. How does knowing that "every single action a person takes has far-reaching consequences" change your self-perception?

2. In this chapter, Jones tells Willow, "If you are [still] alive, then you are still here, physically, on this planet. If you are still here, then you have not completed what you were put on earth to do." How is this a "proof of hope"?

3. It is mentioned in chapter 6 that "every one of us is always in a crisis, coming out of a crisis, or headed for a crisis. That's just part of being on this planet." How can you use this idea to your advantage?

CHAPTER 7

1. How does the "small stuff" contribute to the "big picture"? Is your current perception of "the big picture" leading you to a "desperate life of hurt and darkness"? What steps must you take to readjust your focus on the "small stuff"?

2. Jones explains to Henry what it means to change: "Most people think it takes a long time to change," he says. "It doesn't.

Change is immediate! Instantaneous! It may take a long time to *decide* to change . . . but *change* happens in a heartbeat!" Before reading this, how were your thoughts on change different? What will you change right now?

3. An intention is defined as "an act or instance of determining mentally upon some action or result." What does Jones say about intentions and actions? Why is an intention so reliant on action?

Chapter 8

1. In chapter 8, Jones explains the difference between a choice and a mistake and how both play significant roles in the act of forgiveness. Are there any choices in your past that need to be identified in order to be forgiven? How will you handle this process?

2. Why is it important for Henry to change now, before his son, Caleb, is brought into this world? Do you think Caleb's success will be dependent on the way he is raised by his parents? How can Henry begin to remove the "generational curse"?

3. What is the history of your first name? Did your parents guide you to "fulfilling the promise" of your name? Why or why not?

CHAPTER 9

1. Sitting with Jones in the Chinese restaurant, Andy says, "As I thought of him as 'Garcia,' he appeared quite obviously Hispanic, yet when 'Chen' came to my mind, there was an old Asian man before me." Why is it important that Jones's physical appearance and ethnicity are undefined throughout the book? Do you think his messages would have been as effective had his ethnicity been clearly defined?

2. Why did Jones decide to take Andy back to the Gulf State Park Pier right before he disappeared? Do you think it was just a coincidence that Andy was faced again with the same situation he had experienced many years earlier?

3. The first thing Jones ever said to Andy and the boy Jason at the pier was, "Move into the light." Why was this so important to hear first? What does this mean to you?

CHAPTER 10

1. Jones's last words in his farewell letter were, "The best is yet to come." What does this mean to you? Is it your responsibility while on this earth to create a meaningful future for the next generations to come?

2. He also says, "You must plant your own seeds in the minds and hearts of those you touch. You will honor my memory with your work." How will you begin planting your own seeds? What will be your first step?

3. Jones's worn, brown suitcase was a significant object through-out the book. Was it his intention to leave what was inside a mystery in order to bring everyone in the town together at the end to receive the strong message about the seeds? Why or why not? What other symbolic messages could you gather about the old worn suitcase?

QUESTIONS FOR PERSONAL REFLECTION

1. Can you think of an example or situation where the "little things" really did make a difference in the final outcome? Remember, "the small stuff is what makes up the larger picture of our lives."

2. What does it mean to you to have a "successful life"? Are there important people in your life that you may be neglecting? What is the extra mile you can take to show that you still care?

3. In chapter 5, Jones says, "There is a wonderful filter most of us possess that allows us to determine if a young man or

woman is suitable as a potential life partner . . . Your friends." Will you or did you ask your friends about your potential spouse? Why or why not? Why are your friends so important when deciding on a potential life partner?

4. Do you have a "Jones" in your life? Are you a "Jones" to anyone else? How can you begin to make changes in your life to be more like Jones?

5. How will you share what you've learned in this book with others? Do you think the life lessons taught throughout the book are lessons that everyone should hear at least once in his or her lifetime? How will your life be different now that you have a better understanding of "perspective"?

ANDY ANDREWS, hailed by a *New York Times* reporter as someone who has "quietly become one of the most influential people in America," is a best-selling novelist and in-demand corporate speaker for the world's largest organizations. He has spoken at the request of four different U.S. presidents and at military bases world-wide. Andy is also the author of *The Traveler's Gift*, *The Lost Choice*, *Island of Saints* and *Return to Sawyerton Springs*. He lives in Orange Beach, Alabama, with his wife Polly and their two sons.

IF YOU HAVE ENJOYED THIS BOOK,
HALLMARK WOULD LOVE
TO HEAR FROM YOU.

Please send your comments to:
Hallmark Book Feedback
P.O. Box 419034
Mail Drop 215
Kansas City, MO 64141

Or e-mail us at:
booknotes@hallmark.com